PIANO • VOCAL

HOLLYWOOD MUSICALS YEAR·BY·YEAR

VOLUME 7
1995 TO 2001

The essays about each film, some of which are from the book *Hollywood Musicals Year by Year, 2nd Edition* (Hal Leonard Corporation, 1999), are by Elaine Schmidt.

ISBN 0·634·03169·4

HAL•LEONARD®
CORPORATION

7777 W. BLUEMOUND RD. P.O. BOX 13819 MILWAUKEE, WI 53213

Visit Hal Leonard Online at
www.halleonard.com

Hollywood Musicals Year by Year 1995-2001
Index by Song Title

	SONG	MOVIE
119	Amor de loca juventud	BUENA VISTA SOCIAL CLUB
43	Beautiful Boy (Darling Boy)	MR. HOLLAND'S OPUS
161	Carnival of the Animals	FANTASIA 2000
47	Cole's Song	MR. HOLLAND'S OPUS
5	Colors of the Wind	POCAHONTAS
190	Come What May	MOULIN ROUGE
173	Friends Never Say Goodbye	THE ROAD TO EL DORADO
74	Go the Distance	HERCULES
30	God Help the Outcasts	THE HUNCHBACK OF NOTRE DAME
52	I Believe in You and Me	THE PREACHER'S WIFE
12	If I Never Knew You (Love Theme from POCAHONTAS)	POCAHONTAS
153	My Funny Friend and Me	THE EMPEROR'S NEW GROOVE
197	One Day I'll Fly Away	MOULIN ROUGE
88	Reflection	MULAN
123	Social Club Buena Vista	BUENA VISTA SOCIAL CLUB
36	Someday	THE HUNCHBACK OF NOTRE DAME
167	Someday Out of the Blue (Theme from El Dorado)	THE ROAD TO EL DORADO
21	Steady as the Beating Drum (Main Title)	POCAHONTAS
58	Step by Step	THE PREACHER'S WIFE
93	True to Your Heart	MULAN
133	Two Worlds	TARZAN™
148	When She Loved Me	TOY STORY 2
104	When You Believe	THE PRINCE OF EGYPT
113	Yo Ho Ho and a Bottle of Yum!	THE RUGRATS MOVIE
66	You Were Loved	THE PREACHER'S WIFE
139	You'll Be in My Heart	TARZAN™
25	You've Got a Friend in Me	TOY STORY
181	Your Heart Will Lead You Home	THE TIGGER MOVIE
79	Zero to Hero	HERCULES

Hollywood Musicals Year by Year 1995-2001
Chronological Index

4   POCAHONTAS (1995)
Colors of the Wind 5
If I Never Knew You
   (Love Theme from POCAHONTAS) 12
Steady as the Beating Drum (Main Title) 21

24   TOY STORY (1995)
You've Got a Friend in Me 25

29   THE HUNCHBACK OF NOTRE DAME (1996)
God Help the Outcasts 30
Someday 36

42   MR. HOLLAND'S OPUS (1996)
Beautiful Boy (Darling Boy) 43
Cole's Song 47

51   THE PREACHER'S WIFE (1996)
I Believe in You and Me .52
Step by Step 58
You Were Loved 66

73   HERCULES (1997)
Go the Distance 74
Zero to Hero 79

87   MULAN (1998)
Reflection 88
True to Your Heart 93

103 THE PRINCE OF EGYPT (1998)
When You Believe 104

112 THE RUGRATS MOVIE (1998)
Yo Ho Ho and a Bottle of Yum! 113

118 BUENA VISTA SOCIAL CLUB (1999)
Amor de loca juventud .119
Social Club Buena Vista .123

132 TARZAN™ (1999)
Two Worlds 133
You'll Be in My Heart 139

147 TOY STORY 2 (1999)
When She Loved Me 148

152 THE EMPEROR'S NEW GROOVE (2000)
My Funny Friend and Me 153

160 FANTASIA 2000 (2000)
Carnival of the Animals .161

166 THE ROAD TO EL DORADO (2000)
Friends Never Say Goodbye 173
Someday Out of the Blue
   (Theme from El Dorado) 167

180 THE TIGGER MOVIE (2000)
Your Heart Will Lead You Home 181

189 MOULIN ROUGE (2001)
Come What May 190
One Day I'll Fly Away 197

John Smith and Pocahontas.

POCAHONTAS

Music and Lyrics: Alan Menken and
Stephen Schwartz
Screenplay: Carl Binder, Susannah Grant,
Philip LaZebnik (Andrew Chapman, uncredited)
Produced by: James Pentecost for Walt Disney
Directed by: Mike Gabriel and Eric Goldberg
Voices: Irene Bedard, Mel Gibson, David Ogden
Stiers, John Kassir, Russell Means, Christian Bale,
Linda Hunt, Danny Mann, Billy Connolly,
Joe Baker, Judy Kuhn, John Pomeroy
Songs: "The Virginia Company"; "Steady as the Beating Drum";
"Just Around the Riverbend"; Listen with Your Heart";
"Mine, Mine, Mine"; "Savages"; "Colors of the Wind"
Released: June 1995; 81 minutes

Pocahontas, which premiered on a huge outdoor screen in
New York City's Central Park, tells a sweet tale of fictionalized
history in early America. The twenty-something Pocahontas of
this animated film was actually about eleven years old when
John Smith arrived in her world. In history she did marry an
Englishman, John Rolfe, and traveled to England with him. She
died there while in her early twenties. The film reverses the long-
standing screen images of native Americans as savages and early
explorers as dignified gentlemen—in the extreme. The script has
the explorers as greedy savages, while the Native Americans are
noble, wise folk, living in blissful harmony with the natural world.
Alan Menken won an Academy Award for the score and, with
Stephen Schwartz, a Golden Globe for "Colors of the Wind."
Pocahontas was followed in 1998 by the video sequel
Pocahontas II: Journey to a New World.

Disney ST. Disney Home Video VC.

1995

Colors of the Wind
from Walt Disney's Pocahontas

Music by ALAN MENKEN
Lyrics by STEPHEN SCHWARTZ

You think I'm an ig-no-rant sav-age, and you've been so man-y plac-es, I guess it must be so. But still I can-not see, if the sav-age one is me, how can there be so much that you don't

Moderately

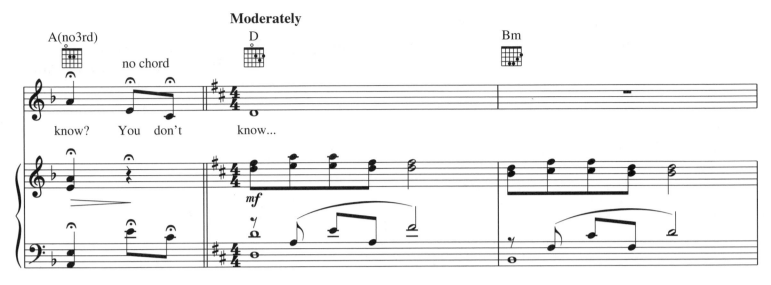

know? You don't know...

You

think you own what-ev-er land you land on; the earth is just a dead thing you can

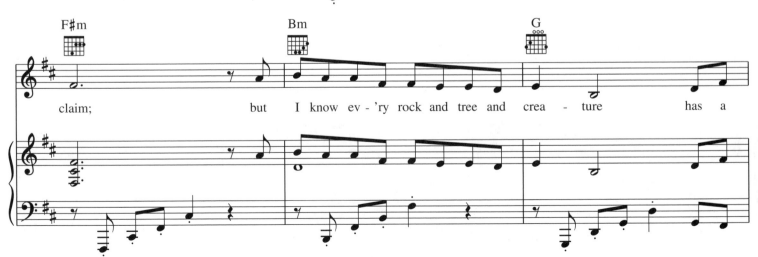

claim; but I know ev-'ry rock and tree and crea - ture has a

life, has a spir-it, has a name. You think the on-ly peo-ple who are

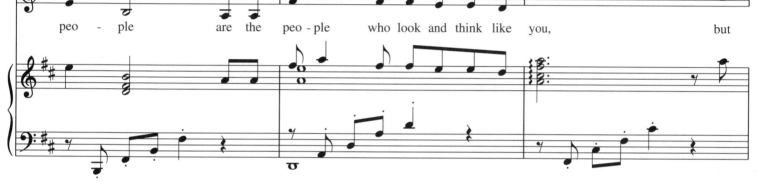

peo - ple are the peo - ple who look and think like you, but

if you walk the foot-steps of a strang – er you'll learn things you nev - er knew you nev - er

knew. _____ Have you ev - er heard the wolf cry to the blue corn moon, or

f *expressively*

for - est, come taste the sun-sweet ber -ries of the earth; come

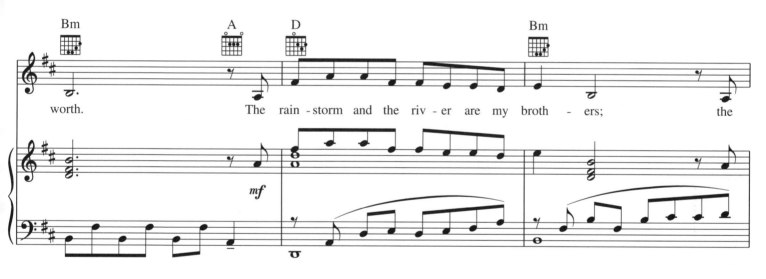

roll in all the rich -es all a -round you, and for once nev -er won -der what they're

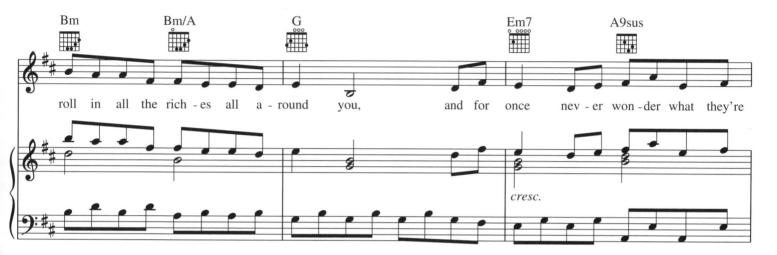

worth. The rain -storm and the riv -er are my broth -ers; the

her -on and the ot -ter are my friends; and we are all con -nect -ed to each

oth - er in a cir - cle, in a hoop that nev - er ends.

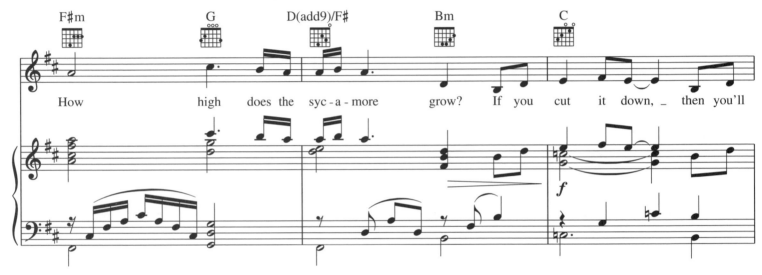

How high does the syc - a - more grow? If you cut it down, _ then you'll

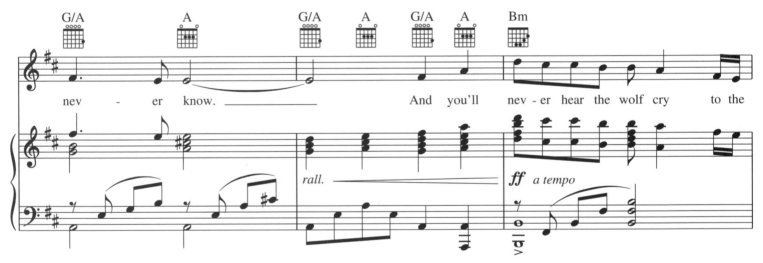

nev - er know. _____ And you'll nev - er hear the wolf cry to the

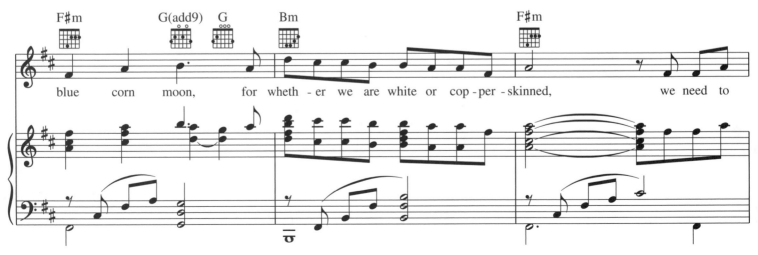

blue corn moon, for wheth - er we are white or cop - per - skinned, we need to

sing with all the voic - es of the moun - tain, need to paint with all the col - ors of the

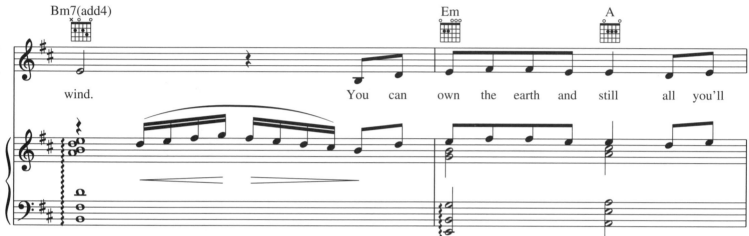

wind. You can own the earth and still all you'll

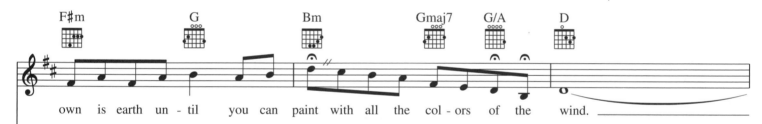

own is earth un - til you can paint with all the col - ors of the wind. _____

If I Never Knew You
(Love Theme from POCAHONTAS)
from Walt Disney's POCAHONTAS

Music by ALAN MENKEN
Lyrics by STEPHEN SCHWARTZ

Moderately slow

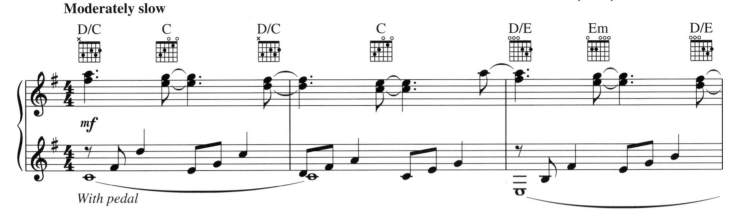

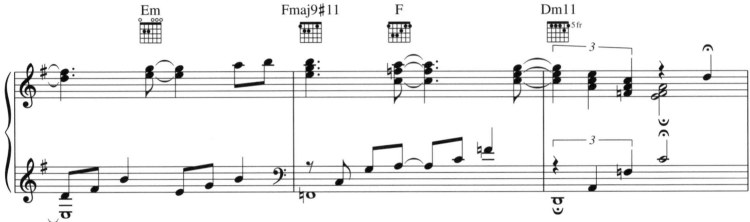

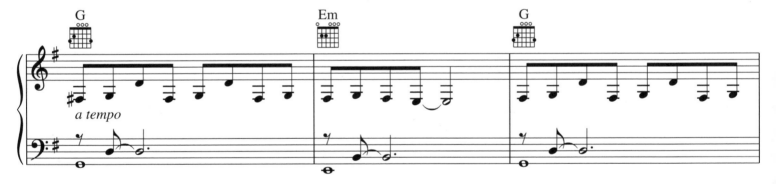

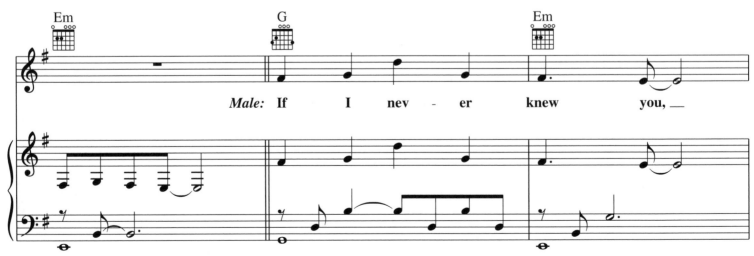

Male: If I nev - er knew you, ___

if I nev - er felt ___ this love, ___ I would have no ink -

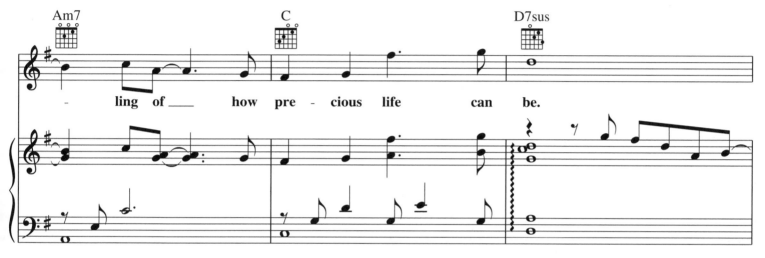

- ling of ___ how pre - cious life can be.

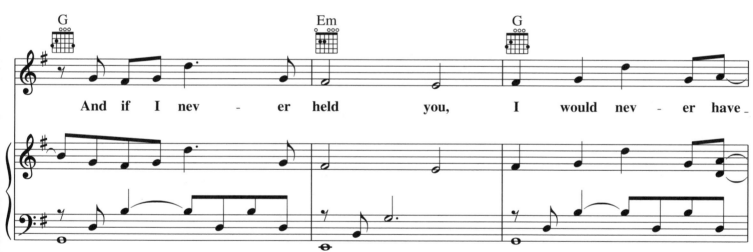

And if I nev - er held you, I would nev - er have ___

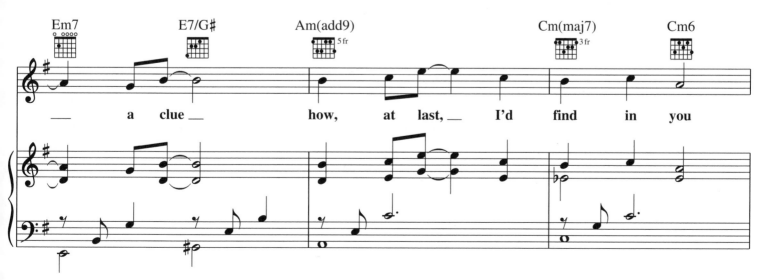

___ a clue ___ how, at last, ___ I'd find in you

Steady as the Beating Drum
(Main Title)
from Walt Disney's POCAHONTAS

Music by ALAN MENKEN
Lyrics by STEPHEN SCHWARTZ

Toy Story

Music and Lyrics: Randy Newman
Screenplay: Joss Wheden, Andrew Stanton,
  Joel Cohen and Alec Skolow; based on a story by
  John Lasseter, Andrew Stanton, Pete Docter
  and Joe Ranft
Produced by: Ralph Guggenheim, Bonnie Arnold
  for Walt Disney
Directed by: John Lasseter (Technicolor)
Voices: Tom Hanks, Tim Allen, Don Rickles,
  Jim Varney, Wallace Shawn, John Ratzenberger,
  Annie Potts, John Morris, Penn Jillette, Erik von Detten,
  Laurie Metcalf, R. Lee Ermey, Sarah Freeman
Songs: "You've Got a Friend in Me"; "Strange Things";
  "I Will Go Sailing No More"
Released: November 1995; 81 minutes

Buzz Lightyear and Woody.

Toy Story was the first feature film created entirely by computer. A child's collection of toys comes to life when no one is looking. They walk and talk and display intricate layers of toy-room politics. Woody (Tom Hanks) is a simple cowboy doll that is the young owner's favorite toy. He reigns as king of the toy hill until a high-tech Buzz Lightyear doll (Tim Allen) arrives as a gift. With the appearance of Buzz, the politics change and Woody is displaced as the favorite. Buzz, however, doesn't realize that he is a toy and works with dogged determination to repair his spaceship (actually the cardboard box in which he was packaged), intending to complete his mission. When the family moves to a new house, Buzz and Woody are marooned at a filling station. They work together to reunite with the family, forging a friendship in the process. Shifting perspectives and toy antics that are unhampered by the laws of physics are all executed in groundbreaking animation. It's just barely a musical, with three fairly incidental songs.

Disney ST. Disney Home Video VC.

1995

You've Got a Friend in Me

FROM WALT DISNEY'S TOY STORY

Music and Lyrics by
RANDY NEWMAN

Easy Shuffle

Eb   G7/D   Cm   B7   Eb/Bb   Ebdim/Bb   Bb7

f

Eb   D/Bb   Db/Bb   D/Bb   Eb   Bb7#5

mf

You've got a friend in me. _
You've got a friend in me. _

Eb9   Ab   Adim7   Eb/Bb   Eb

You've got a friend in me. __
You've got a friend in me. __

Ab   Eb/G   G7   Cm

When the road __ looks rough a-head __ and you're miles _
You got trou-bles, then I got 'em too. __

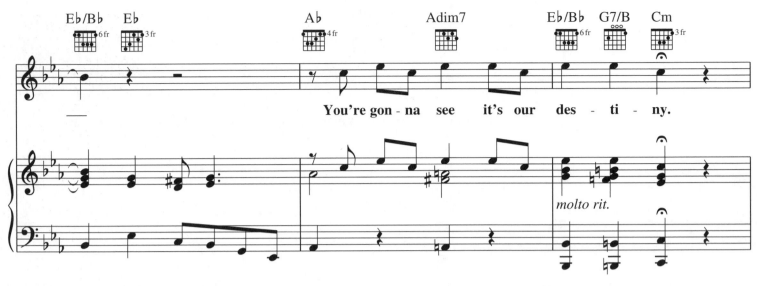

The Hunchback of Notre Dame

Music and Lyrics: Alan Menken and
Stephen Schwartz
Screenplay: Irene Mecchi, after the novel by
Victor Hugo
Produced by: Roy Conti, Don Hahn
Directed by: Gary Trousdale, Kirk Wise
for Walt Disney
Cast: Tom Hulce, Demi Moore, Tony Jay, Kevin Kline,
Paul Kandel, Jason Alexander, Charles Kimbrough,
Mary Wickes, David Ogden Stiers, Heidi Mollenhauer
Songs: "The Bells of Notre Dame"; "Out There"; "God Help the
Outcasts"; "Heaven's Light"; "Hellfire"; "A Guy Like You";
"The Court of Miracles"; "Someday"; "Topsy Turvy"
Released: June 1996; 91 minutes

The Hunchback of Notre Dame.

Disney both followed and broke its own model for animated success with *The Hunchback of Notre Dame*. A plucky heroine appears in the form of the gypsy Esmeralda (Demi Moore), and she finds love and happiness before the end of the tale. But in this story the young woman rescues her man, Phoebus (Kevin Kline), and breaks the heart of the suffering hunchback Quasimodo (Tom Hulce), who also has fallen in love with her. Also in love with her, and hating himself for loving a gypsy, is the evil Judge Frollo (Tony Jay). There is a happy ending, but a qualified one, as the poor, disfigured Quasimodo finds affection but not romantic love. The darkness and layers of this story are beautifully set in a cathedral that is as much a character in the story as a backdrop to it. Director Gary Trousdale appears as the voice of the Old Heretic. Bette Midler sings the final reprise of "God Help the Outcasts." The pop vocal group All-4-One had a hit single with "Someday."

Walt Disney ST. Walt Disney Home Video VC.

1996

God Help the Outcasts

FROM WALT DISNEY'S THE HUNCHBACK OF NOTRE DAME

Music by ALAN MENKEN
Lyrics by STEPHEN SCHWARTZ

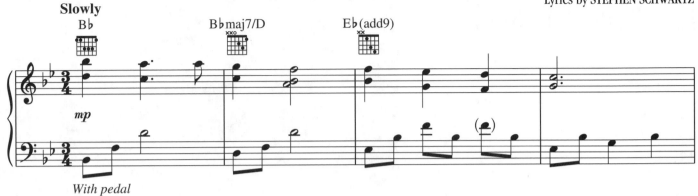

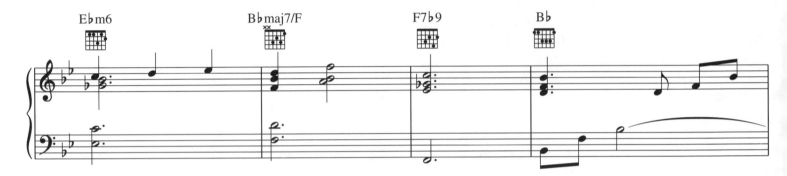

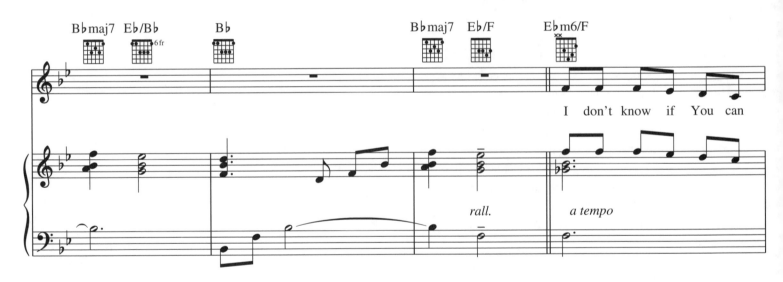

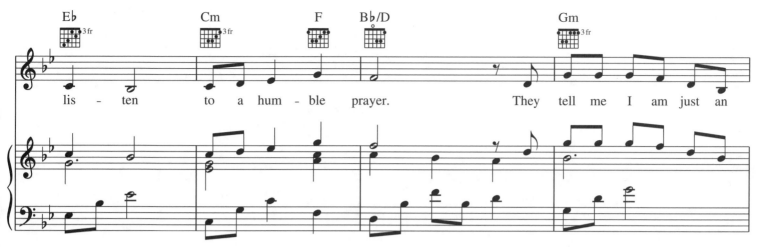

lis - ten to a hum - ble prayer. They tell me I am just an

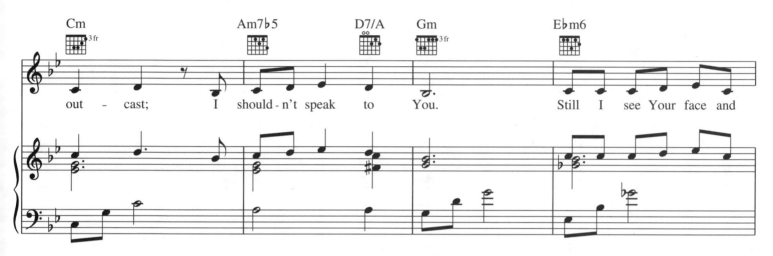

out - cast; I should - n't speak to You. Still I see Your face and

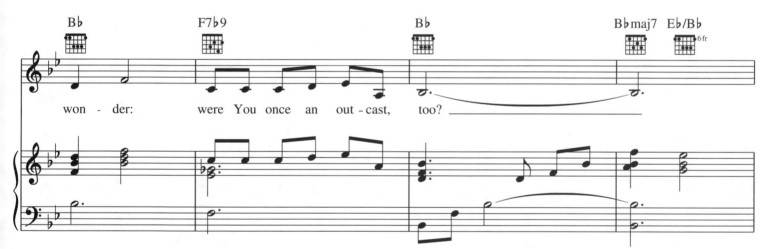

won - der: were You once an out - cast, too? _____

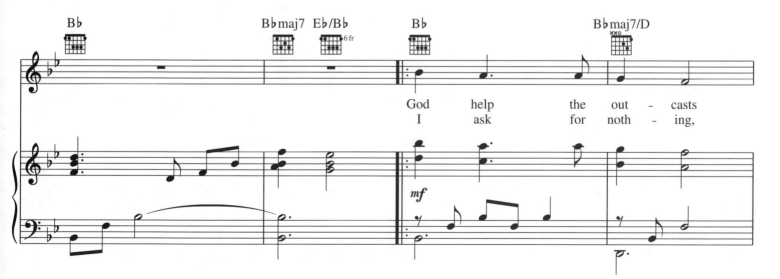

God help the out - casts
I ask for noth - ing,

hun - gry from birth. Show them the mer - cy they
I can get by. But I know so man - y less

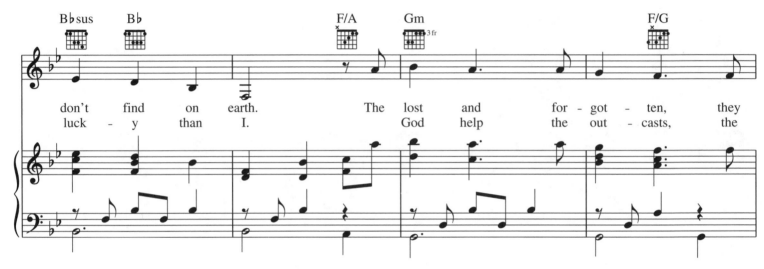

don't find on earth. The lost and for - got - ten, they
luck - y than I. God help the out - casts, the

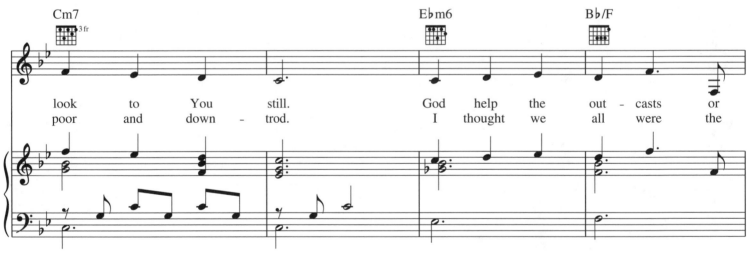

look to You still. God help the out - casts or
poor and down - trod. I thought we all were the

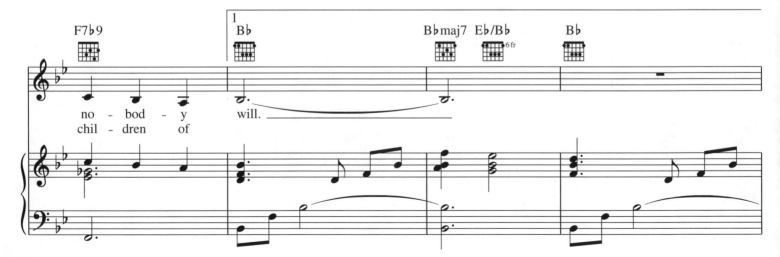

no - bod - y will. _____
chil - dren of

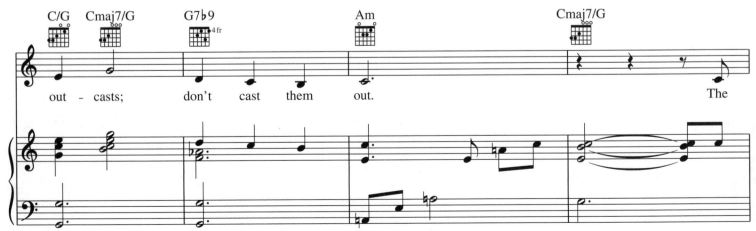

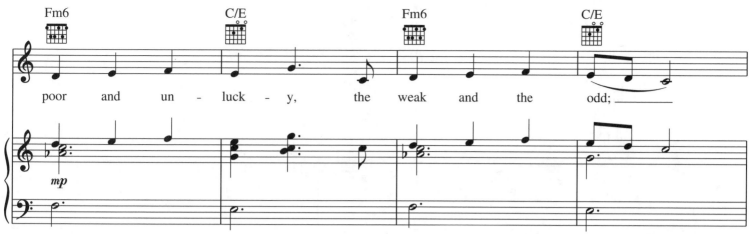

poor and un - luck - y, the weak and the odd; _____

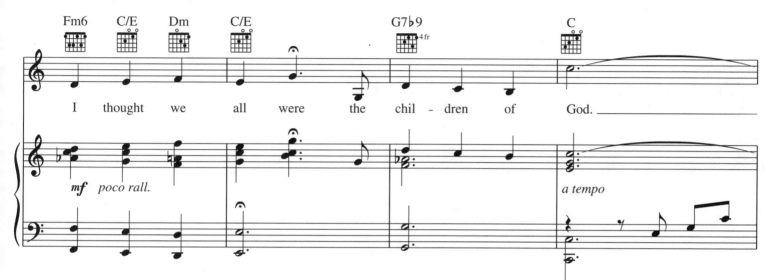

I thought we all were the chil - dren of God. _____

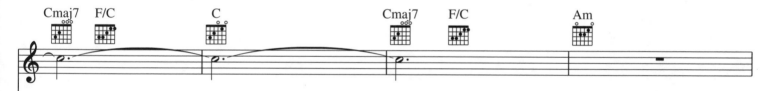

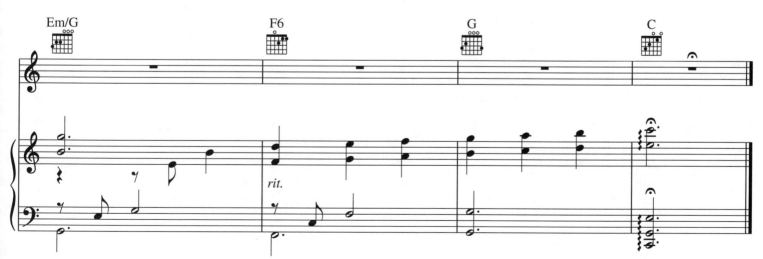

Someday

from Walt Disney's The Hunchback of Notre Dame

Music by ALAN MENKEN
Lyrics by STEPHEN SCHWARTZ

Some - day when we are wis - er, when the world's

old - er, when we have learned,

I pray some-day we may yet live _____ to

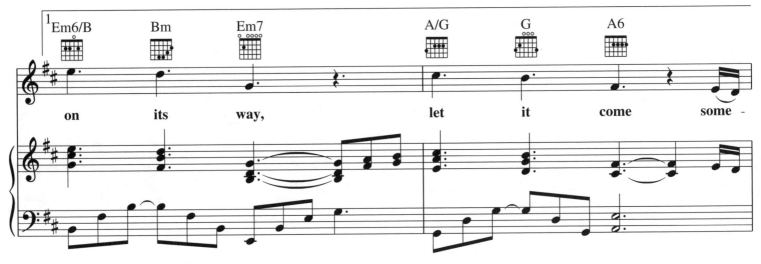

on its way, let it come some -

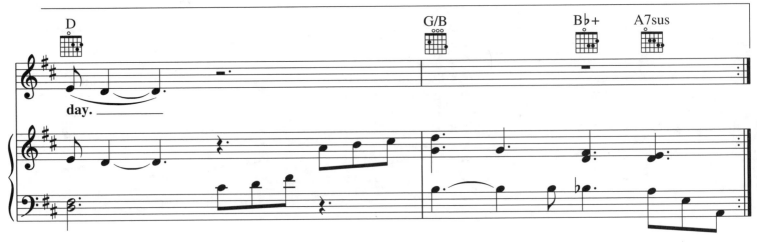

day. ____

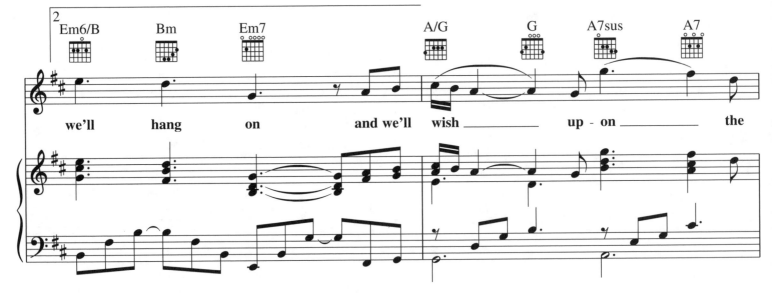

we'll hang on and we'll wish _____ up - on _____ the

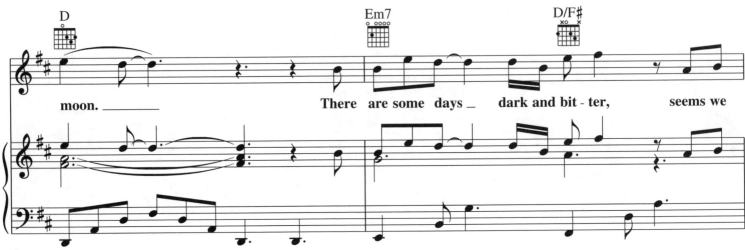

moon. _____ There are some days _ dark and bit - ter, seems we

have - n't got a prayer, ___ but a prayer for some-day bet - ter ___ is the

one thing we all share. _____ Some - day when we are

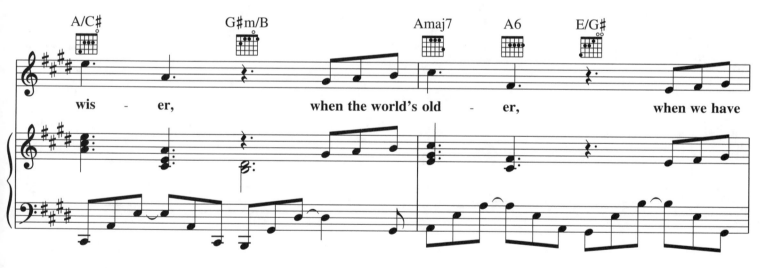

wis - er, when the world's old - er, when we have

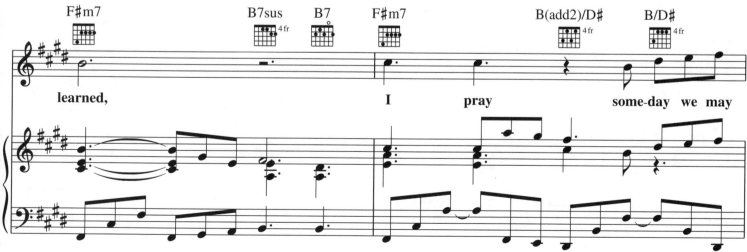

learned, I pray some-day we may

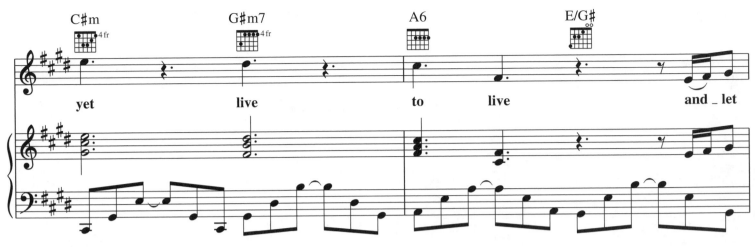

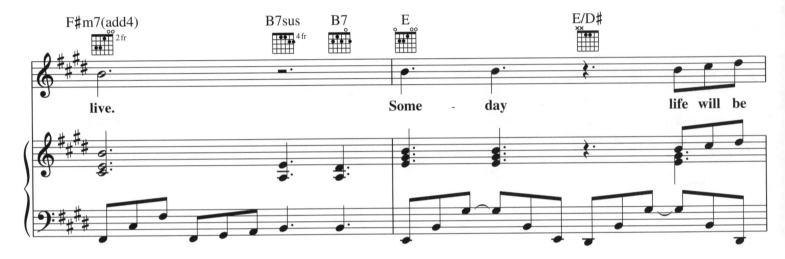

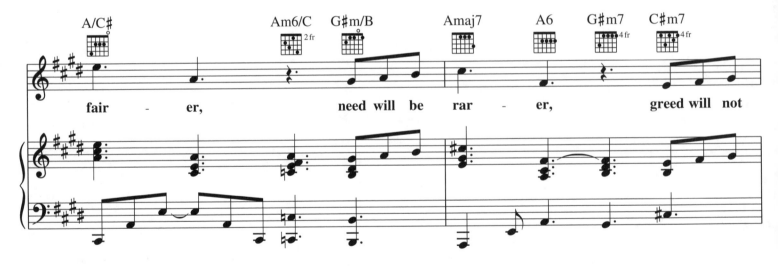

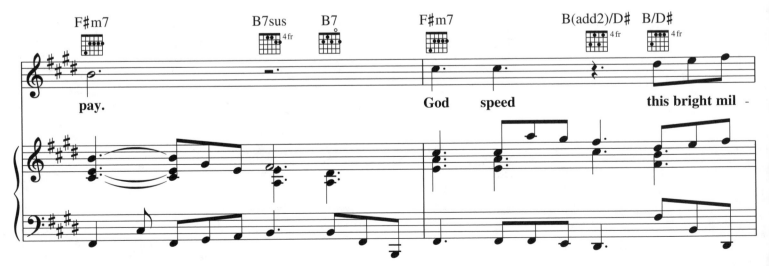

len - ni - um, let it come

wish up - on _____ the moon. ___ One day, some - day ___

soon. ___

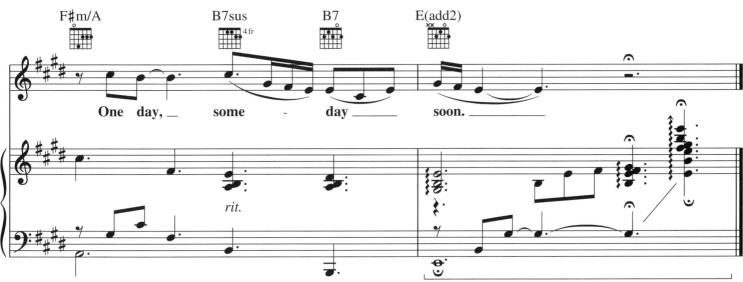

One day, ___ some - day ___ soon. ___

Mr. Holland's Opus

Music: Michael Kamen, various
Screenplay: Patrick Sheane Duncan
Produced by: Robert W. Cort, Ted Field,
   Michael Nolin
Directed by: Stephen Herek for Buena
   Vista/Hollywood Pictures
Photography: Oliver Wood (Technicolor)
Cast: Richard Dreyfuss, Glenne Headly, Jay Thomas,
   Olympia Dukakis, W. H. Macy, Alicia Witt, Terrence
   Howard, Damon Whitaker, Jean Louisa Kelly,
   Alexandra Boyd
Songs: "Cole's Song" (Michael Kamen, Julian Lennon and
   Justin Clayton); "Beautiful Boy" (John Lennon);
   "An American Symphony (Mr. Holland's Opus)"; "Louie
   Louie" (Richard Berry); "Someone to Watch Over Me"
   (George and Ira Gershwin)
Released: January 1996; 143 minutes

Richard Dreyfuss.

In telling the story of a high school music teacher's thirty-year career, *Mr. Holland's Opus* became a manifesto for the continuation of arts programs in American public schools. Holland (Richard Dreyfuss) has reluctantly given up a life on the road and aspirations to be a composer for marrying and settling down. A surprise pregnancy seals his fate. Holland blossoms as a teacher, but is dealt an ironic blow by having a deaf son. As the decades pass, complete with occasional evening-news clips, Holland's various students leave. One seeks a stage career in New York, one dies in Viet Nam and another becomes governor of the state. After thirty years, but still too soon for his retirement, the school district eliminates the music program for budgetary reasons, throwing Holland out of a job. On the day he packs to leave the school he is given a tribute before a cheering auditorium filled with his former students. (With all that support, especially with the governor there, you would think it would have saved the music budget and Holland's job; but then it would lose the Hollywood melodrama.) Many of the former high-school musicians take the stage and miraculously, without rehearsal, perform the piece he has been composing for several years, "Mr. Holland's Opus."

Polygram ST. Hollywood Pictures VC.

Beautiful Boy
(Darling Boy)
FROM MR. HOLLAND'S OPUS

Words and Music by
JOHN LENNON

Close your eyes, __ have no fear. __ The
go to sleep, __ say a lit - tle prayer. __

mon - ster's gone. __ He's on the run, __ and your dad - dy's here. __
Ev - 'ry day, __ in ev - 'ry way, __ it's get - ting bet - ter and bet - ter.

to see you come of age.____ But I guess we'll both__

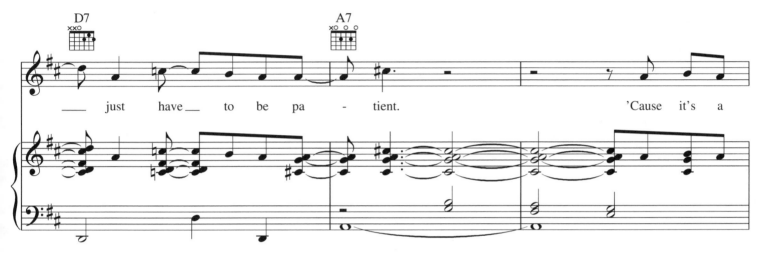

____ just have__ to be pa - tient. 'Cause it's a

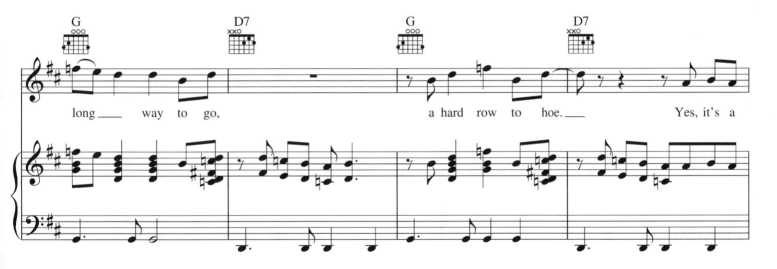

long____ way to go, a hard row to hoe.____ Yes, it's a

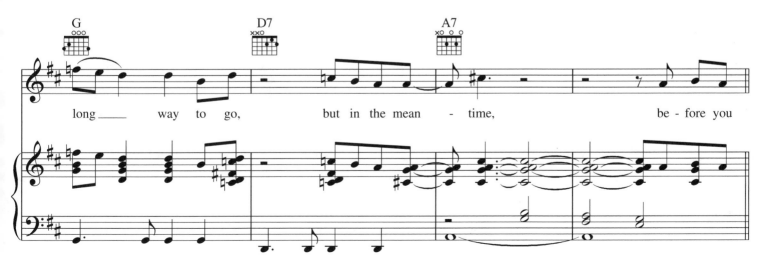

long____ way to go, but in the mean - time, be - fore you

Cole's Song

FROM MR. HOLLAND'S OPUS

Words by JULIAN LENNON and JUSTIN CLAYTON
Music by MICHAEL KAMEN

THE PREACHER'S WIFE

Music and Lyrics: Various
Screenplay: Allan Scott, Nat Mauldin and Todd Graff
(uncredited). Based on *The Bishop's Wife* by Leonardo
Bercovici and Robert E. Sherwood.
Produced by: Samuel Goldwyn Jr. for Touchstone Pictures
and the Samuel Goldwyn Company.
Directed by: Penny Marshall
Photography: Miroslav Ondricek (Technicolor)
Cast: Whitney Houston, Denzel Washington, Courtney B. Vance,
Gregory Hines, Jenifer Lewis, Loretta Devine, Lionel Richie,
Paul Bates, Justin Pierre Edmund, Lex Monson, Darvel Davis
Jr., William James Stiggers Jr., Marcella Lowery, Cissy Houston,
Aaron A. McConnaughey
Songs: "Somebody Bigger Than You and I" (Johnny Lange,
Hy Heath and Sonny Burke); "Lay Aside Every Weight"
(Glenn Burleigh); Hold On, Help Is on the Way"
(Rev. Kenneth Paden); "You Were Loved" (Diane Warren);
"Who Would Imagine a King" (Mervyn Warren, Hallerin
Hilton Hill); "My Heart Is Calling" (Kenneth "Babyface"
Edwards); "I Believe in You and Me" (David Wolfert,
Sandy Linzer); "I Love the Lord" (Richard Smallwood);
"Step by Step" (Annie Lennox)
Released: December 1996; 124 minutes

Whitney Houston.

The Preacher's Wife, a light, Merry Christmas comedy, is a remake of the 1947 *The Bishop's Wife*, which starred Cary Grant, David Niven and Loretta Young. A preacher (Courtney B. Vance) struggles to hold together both the souls and aging building of his inner city church. In the process he overlooks the needs of his wife (Whitney Houston) and son. An angel named Dudley (Denzel Washington) drops in to put things right. The film toys with a possible romance between the preacher's wife and the angel, as the angel rediscovers the physical world he has left behind. In the end he does his job, setting the preacher and his wife back on the right track. A sub-plot of the film makes Houston a former nightclub singer who now sings only in church. That seemingly minor plot point allows for some fine gospel singing from Houston, backed by a rousing gospel choir, and one scene in a nightclub where she sings "I Believe in You and Me." That song became the movie's big hit.

BMG/Arista ST. Touchstone Home Video ST.

I Believe in You and Me

FROM THE TOUCHSTONE MOTION PICTURE THE PREACHER'S WIFE

Words and Music by DAVID WOLFERT
and SANDY LINZER

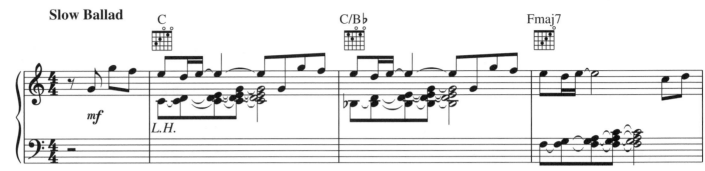

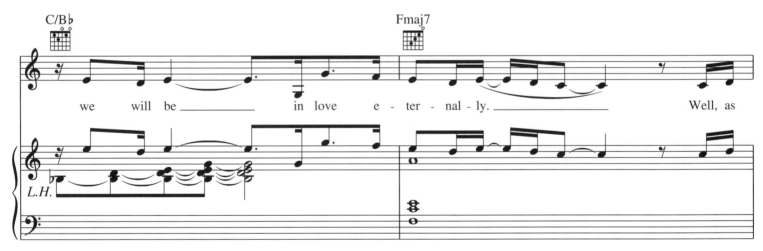

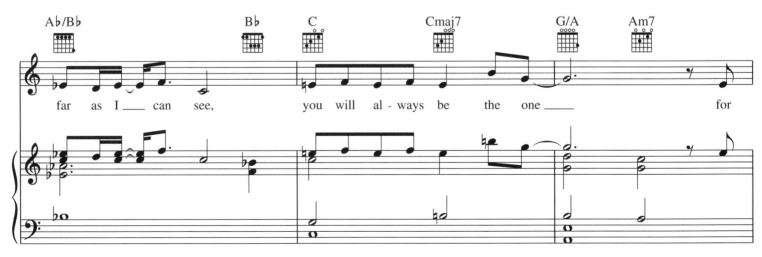

me, _____ oh, yes, you will. And I be-lieve in dreams _

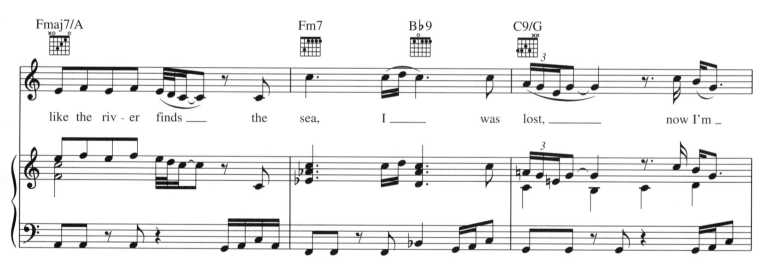

___ a - gain. _____ I be-lieve that love will nev-er end. _____ And

like the riv-er finds ___ the sea, I ___ was lost, _____ now I'm _

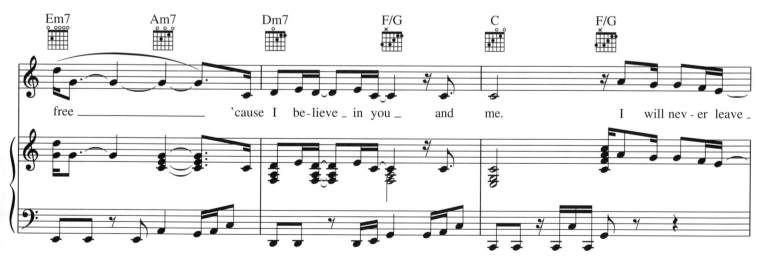

free _____ 'cause I be-lieve _ in you _ and me. I will nev-er leave _

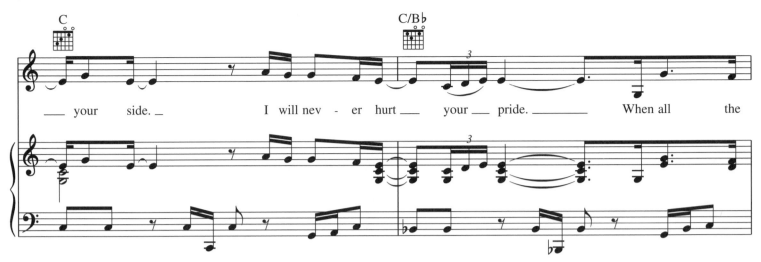

your side. I will nev - er hurt your pride. When all the

chips are down, babe, then I will al - ways be a - round.

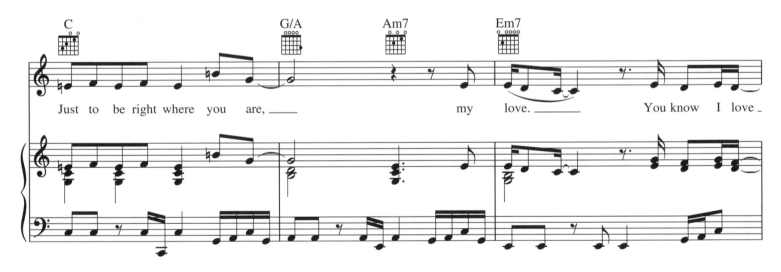

Just to be right where you are, my love. You know I love

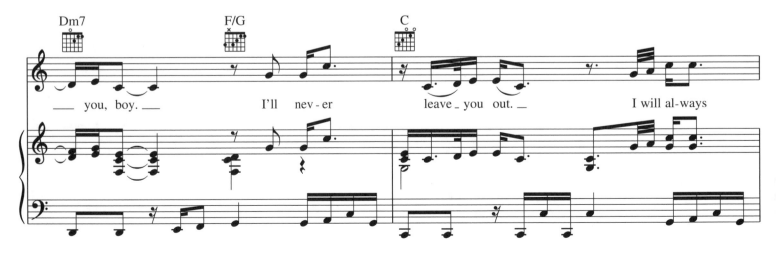

you, boy. I'll nev - er leave you out. I will al - ways

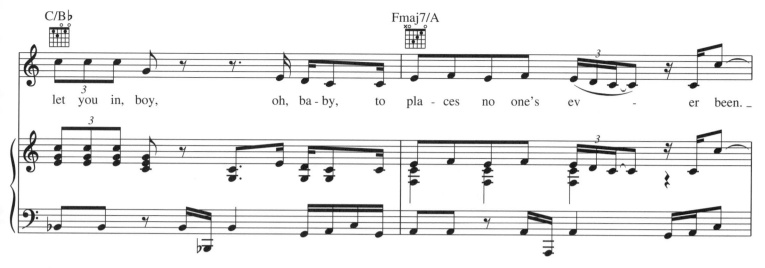

let you in, boy, oh, ba-by, to pla-ces no one's ev - er been. _

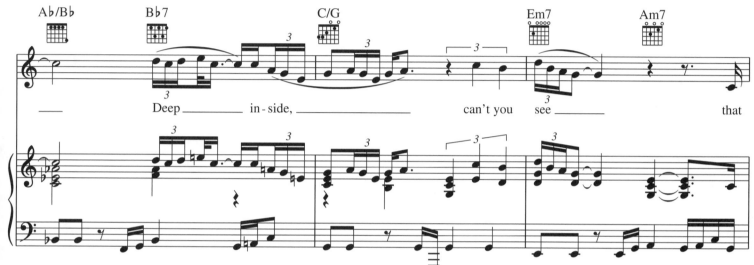

_ Deep _____ in-side, _____ can't you see _____ that

I be-lieve _ in you _____ and me. May-be I'm a fool _____ to

feel the way _ I do. _____ I would play _____ the fool for-ev - er _____

I be-lieve, _ I do be-lieve in you and me. See, I'm _

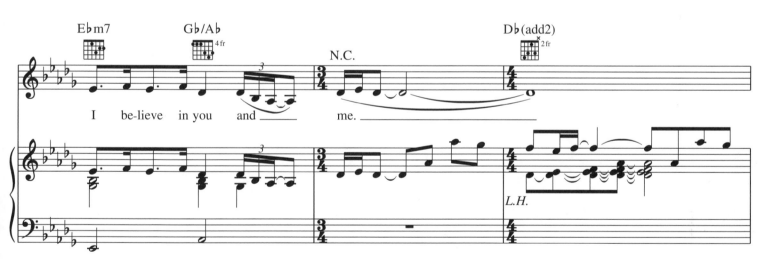

lost, _____ now I'm free _____ 'cause

I be-lieve in you and _____ me. _____

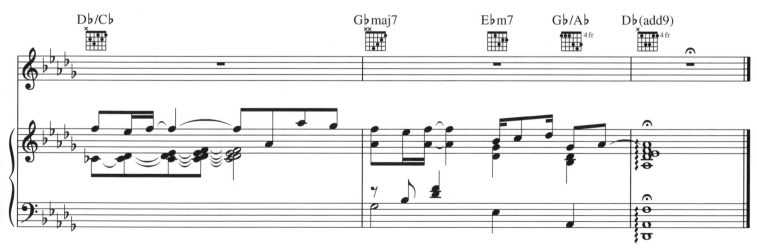

Step by Step

from the Touchstone Motion Picture THE PREACHER'S WIFE

Words and Music by
ANNIE LENNOX

Steady dance beat

Well, there's a bridge and there's a riv-er that I still must cross

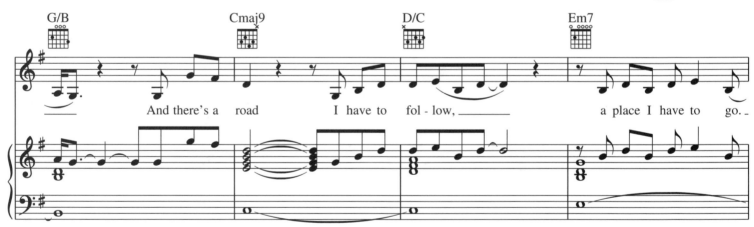

as I'm go-ing on my jour-ney, though I might be lost.

And there's a road I have to fol-low, a place I have to go.

Well, no one told me just how to get there, but when I get there I'll know.

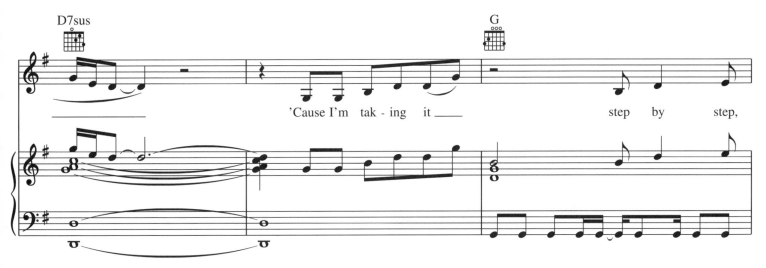

'Cause I'm tak-ing it _____ step by step,

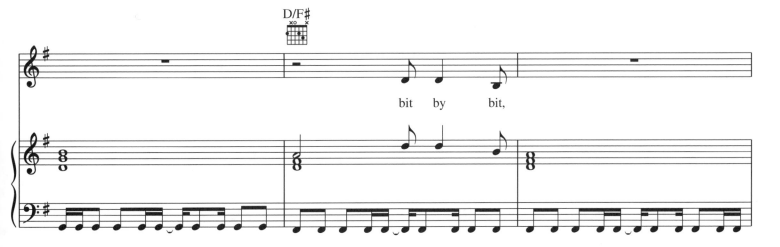

bit by bit,

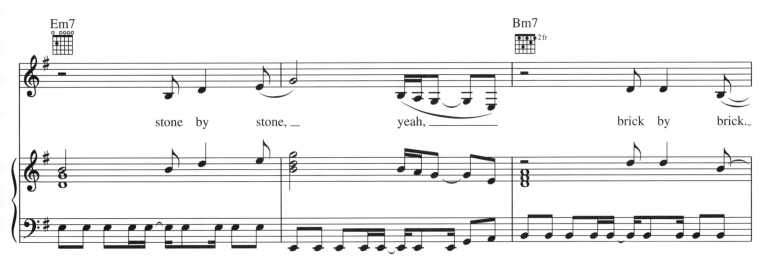

stone by stone, _____ yeah, _____ brick by brick. _____

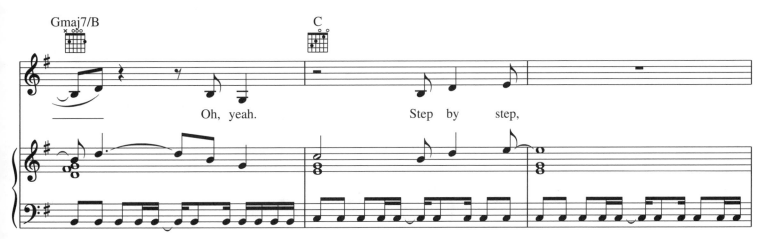

Oh, yeah. Step by step,

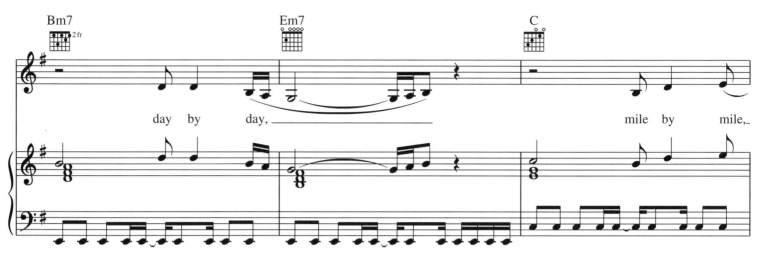

day by day, _____ mile by mile,_

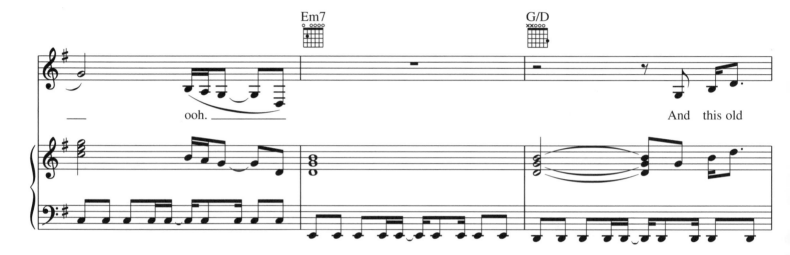

_ ooh. _____ And this old

road is rough in ru - in, so man-y dan - gers a - long_ the way._

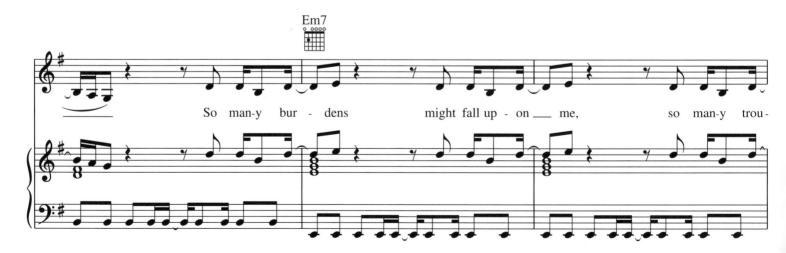

_____ So man-y bur - dens might fall up - on ___ me, so man-y trou-

-bles that I have to face. ___ Oh, ___ but I won't let ___ my spir-it fail ___

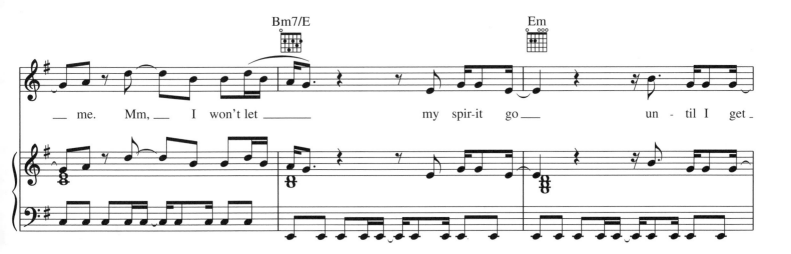

___ me. Mm, ___ I won't let _____ my spir-it go ___ un - til I get ___

___ to my des - ti-na - tion. ___ I'm gon - na take ___ it slow ___

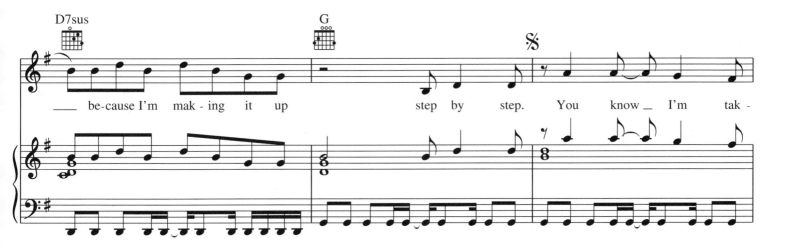

___ be-cause I'm mak-ing it up step by step. You know ___ I'm tak -

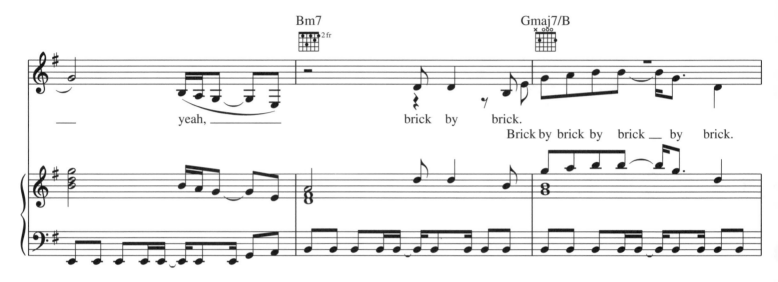

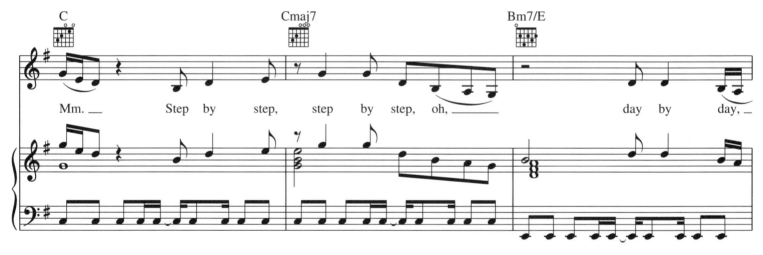

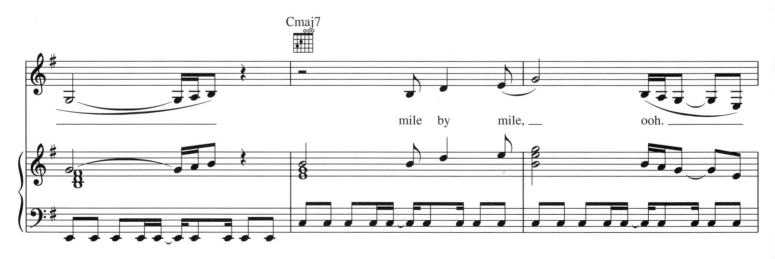

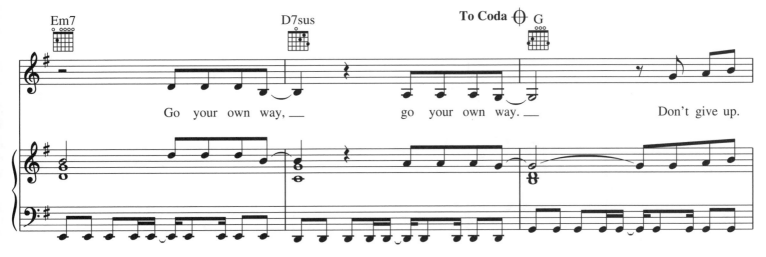

Go your own way, ___ go your own way. ___ Don't give up.

You've got to hold on to what you've ___ got. _____ Oh, ___ ba-

by, don't give up. You've got to keep on ___ mov - in', don't

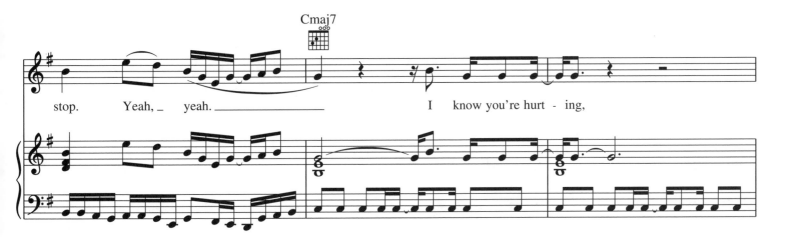

stop. Yeah, _ yeah. _____ I know you're hurt - ing,

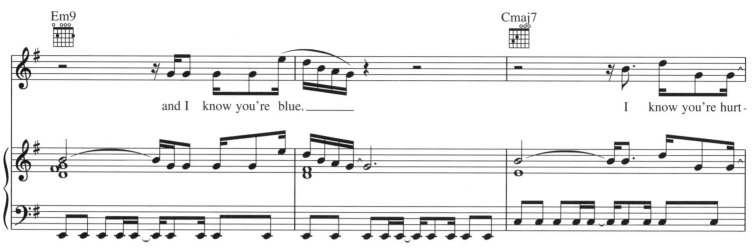

and I know you're blue._____

Cmaj7

I know you're hurt-

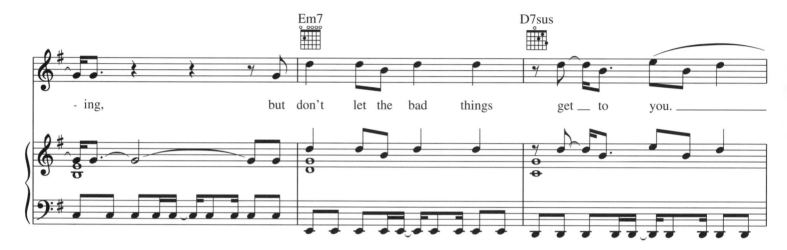

-ing, but don't let the bad things get _ to you._____

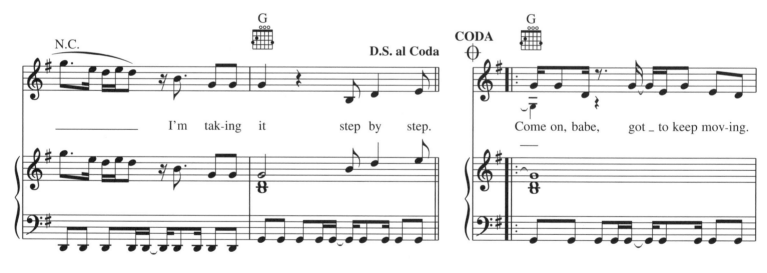

N.C. G D.S. al Coda CODA G

_____ I'm tak-ing it step by step. Come on, babe, got _ to keep mov-ing.

D/F#

Come on, babe, got _ to keep mov-ing. Come on, babe, got _ to keep mov-in'. Come on, babe, got _ to keep mov-in'.
(Bit by bit.)

You Were Loved

FROM THE TOUCHSTONE MOTION PICTURE THE PREACHER'S WIFE

Words and Music by
DIANE WARREN

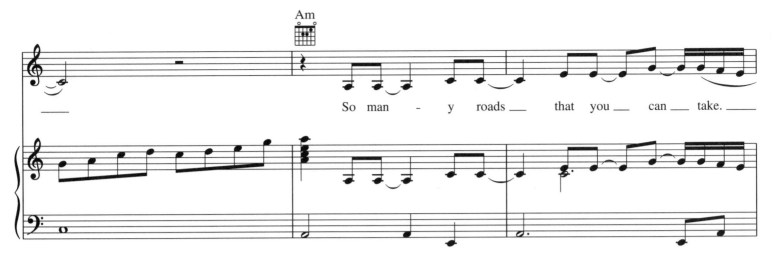

So man - y roads _____ that you _____ can _____ take. _____

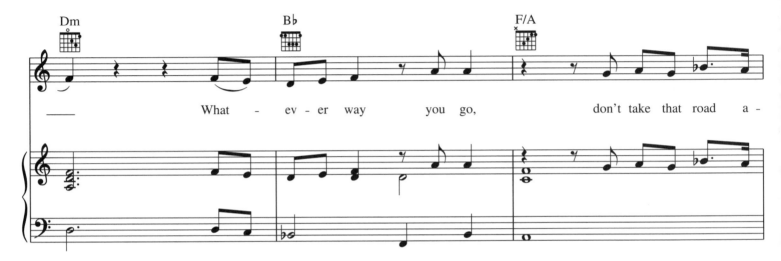

_____ What - ev - er way you go, don't take that road a -

lone. _____ It's bet - ter you should know _____ you

are _____ loved by some - one, touched by some - one,

HERCULES

Music and Lyrics: Alan Menken and David Zippel
Screenplay: Ron Clements, Donald McEnery, Bob Shaw, Irene Mecchi
Produced by: Alice Dewey, John Musker, Ron Clements
Directed by: John Musker, Ron Clements
Cast: Tate Donovan, Joshua Keaton, Roger Bart, Danny DeVito, James Woods, Susan Eagan, Bob Goldthwaite, Matt Frewer, Rip Torn, Samantha Eggar, Barbara Barrie, Hal Holbrook
Songs: "One Last Hope"; "Go the Distance"; "The Gospel Truth"; "A Star Is Born"; "I Won't Say (I'm in Love)"; "Zero to Hero"
Released: June 1997; 92 minutes

Hercules.

With *Hercules*, Disney made a return to the lighter musical comedy fare of its earlier animated musicals. Gone are the serious tones of *Pocahontas*, *The Hunchback of Notre Dame* and *The Lion King*. *Hercules* is a happy, snappy Disney romp through Greek mythology. Yes, the young Hercules grows up and finds love in very Disney fashion, but he does it with the help of a doting Pegasus and a diminutive satyr named Phil (Danny DeVito). Hercules (Tate Donovan) is half man/half deity and all teenager, tripping over his too-big feet and trashing entire structures in the process with his unbridled strength. He learns that he is the son of Zeus (Rip Torn) and must prove himself a true hero to regain his place among the other deities. "Herc" performs a laundry list of heroic feats, but it is in risking his own life to save Meg (Susan Eagan) that he wins back his birthright. He then gives it up to remain on earth with her as a mortal. Charlton Heston is also heard on the soundtrack. Singer Michael Bolton scored a hit with "Go the Distance."

Disney ST. Disney Home Video VC.

Go the Distance

FROM WALT DISNEY PICTURES' HERCULES
AS PERFORMED BY MICHAEL BOLTON

Music by ALAN MENKEN
Lyrics by DAVID ZIPPEL

Slowly

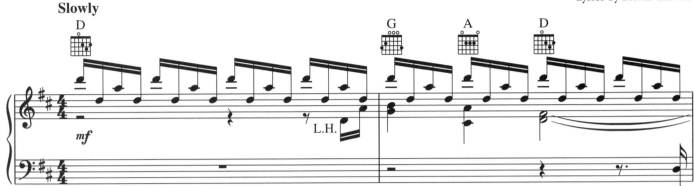

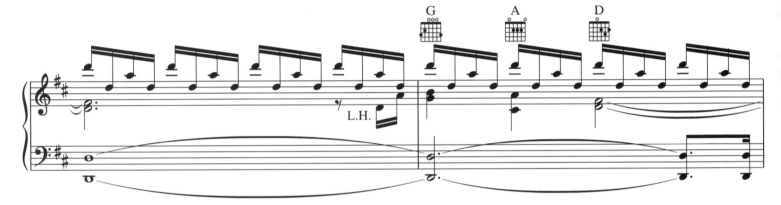

I have of-ten dreamed of a far-off place, where a
un-known road to em-brace my fate, though that

he - ro's wel-come would be wait - ing for me, where the crowds will cheer when they
road may wan-der, it will lead me to you. And a thou - sand years would be

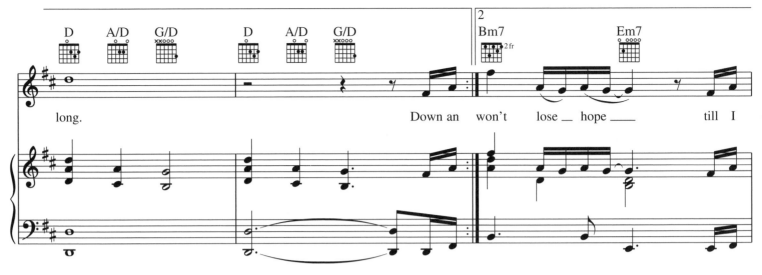

long. Down an won't lose __ hope ____ till I

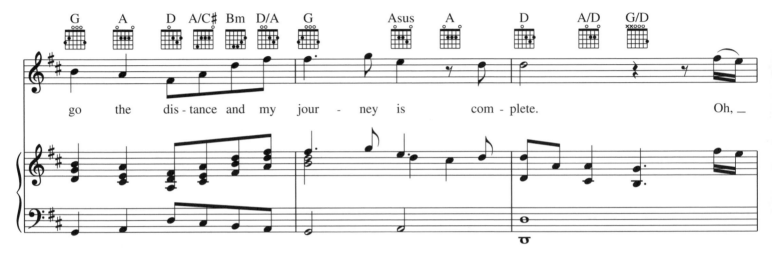

go the dis - tance and my jour - ney is com - plete. Oh, __

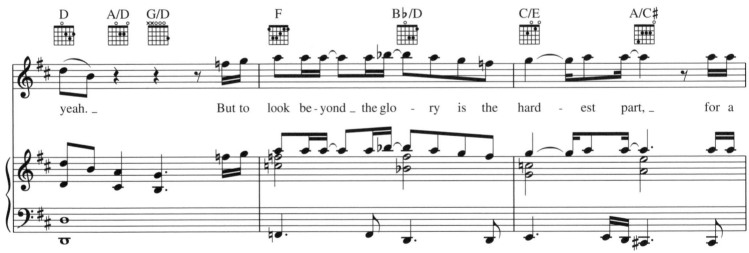

yeah. __ But to look be - yond __ the glo - ry is the hard - est part, __ for a

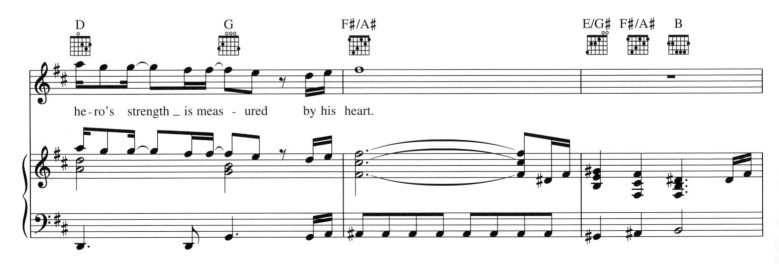

he - ro's strength __ is meas - ured by his heart.

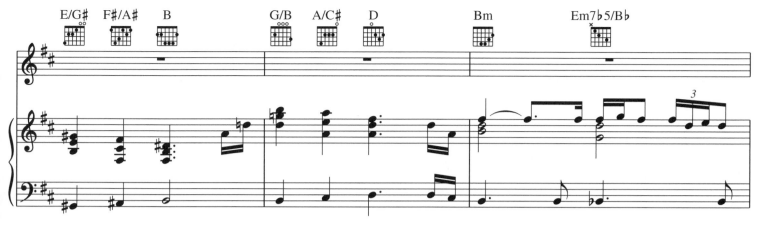

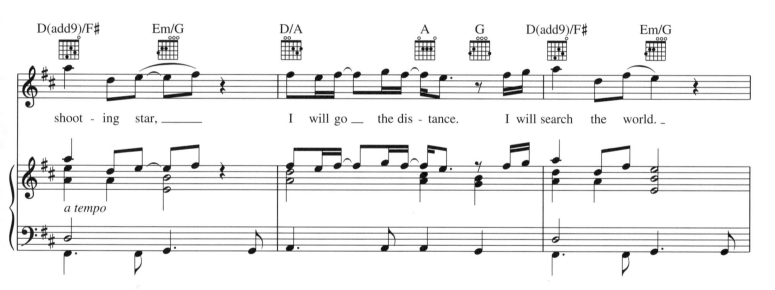

shoot - ing star, _____ I will go __ the dis - tance. I will search the world. _

I will face _ its harms. I _____ don't care how far. _____ I can go the dis - tance till I

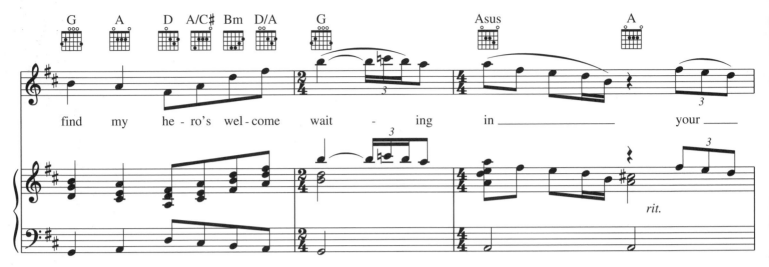

find my he-ro's wel-come wait - ing in _____ your _____

Broadly

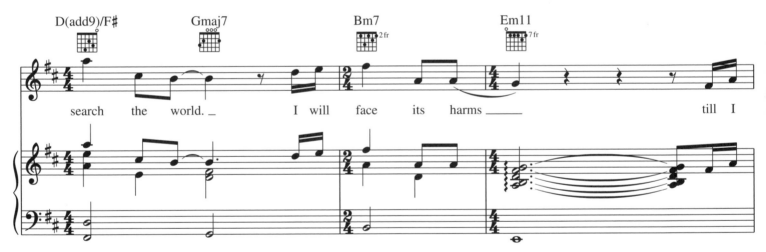

arms. I will

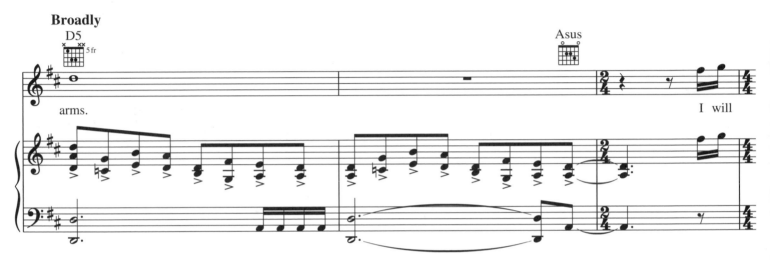

search the world. _ I will face its harms _____ till I

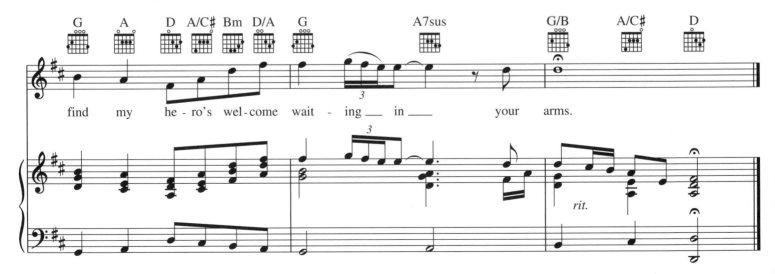

find my he-ro's wel-come wait - ing ___ in ___ your arms.

Zero to Hero

FROM WALT DISNEY PICTURES' HERCULES

Music by ALAN MENKEN
Lyrics by DAVID ZIPPEL

Driving 4

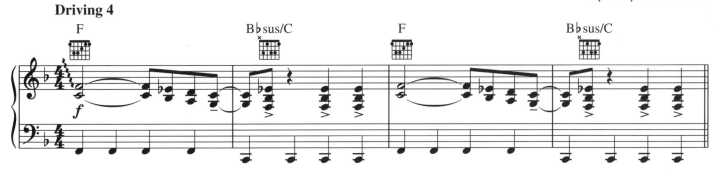

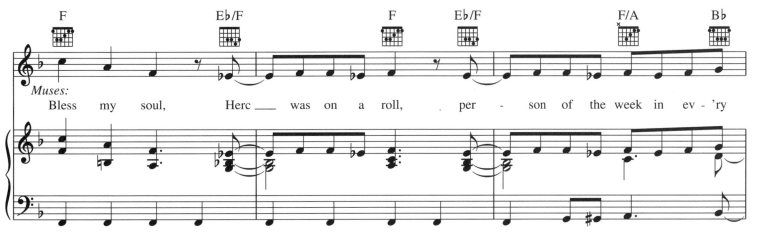

Muses:
Bless my soul, Herc ___ was on a roll, per - son of the week in ev - 'ry

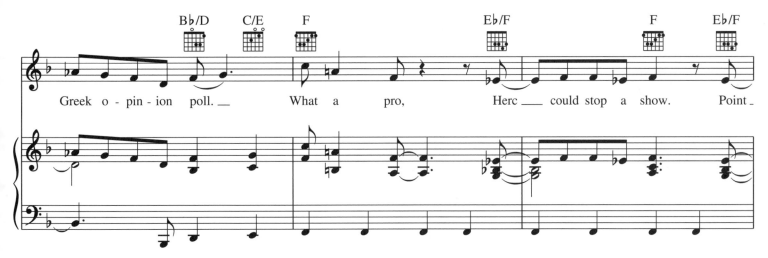

Greek o - pin - ion poll. ___ What a pro, Herc ___ could stop a show. Point ___

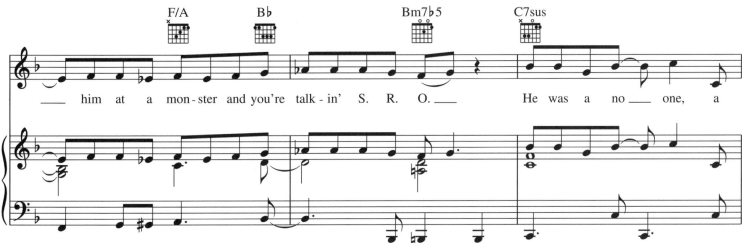

___ him at a mon - ster and you're talk - in' S. R. O. ___ He was a no ___ one, a

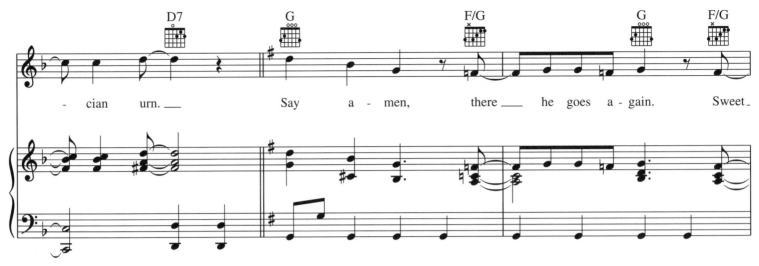

-cian urn. __ Say a-men, there __ he goes a-gain. Sweet __

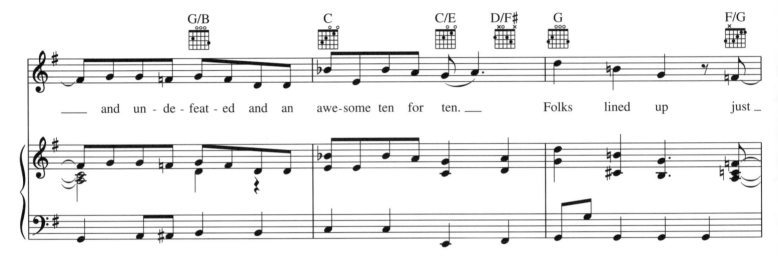

__ and un-de-feat-ed and an awe-some ten for ten. __ Folks lined up just __

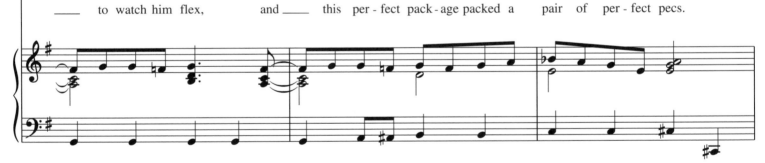

__ to watch him flex, and __ this per-fect pack-age packed a pair of per-fect pecs.

Herc-ie, he comes, _ he sees, __ he con-quers. Hon-ey, the crowds _ were go-

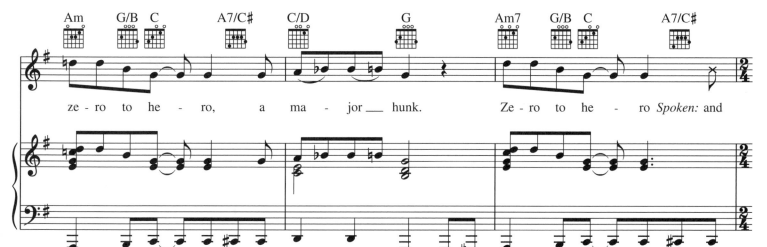

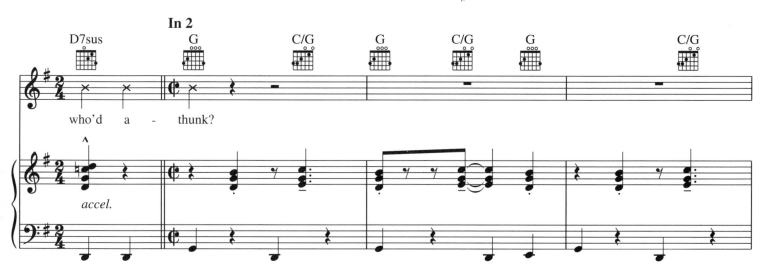

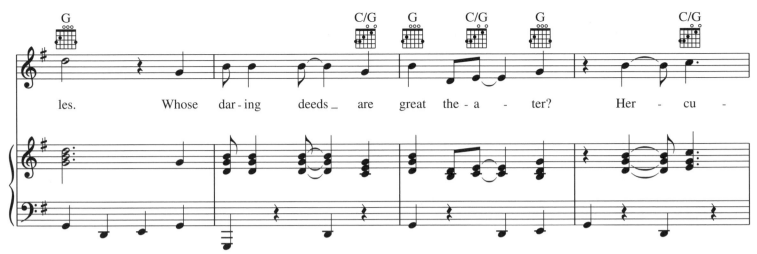

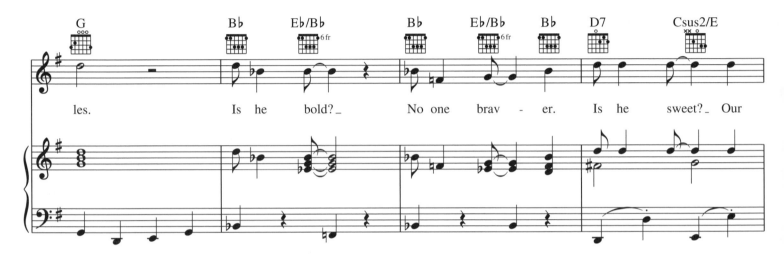

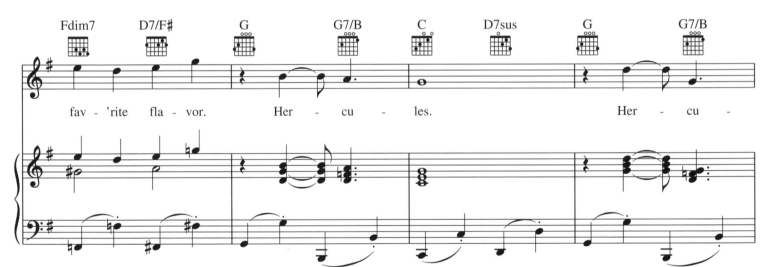

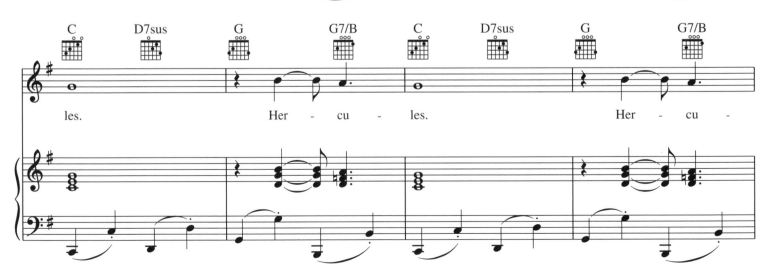

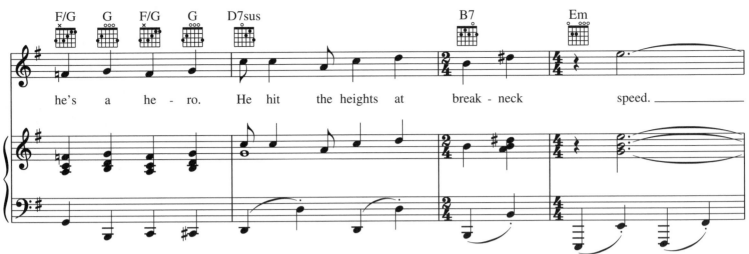

he's a he-ro. He hit the heights at break-neck speed.

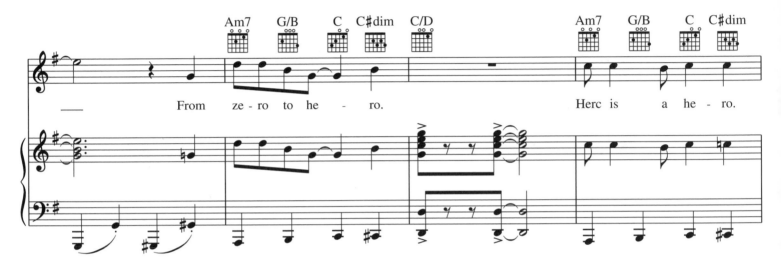

From ze-ro to he-ro. Herc is a he-ro.

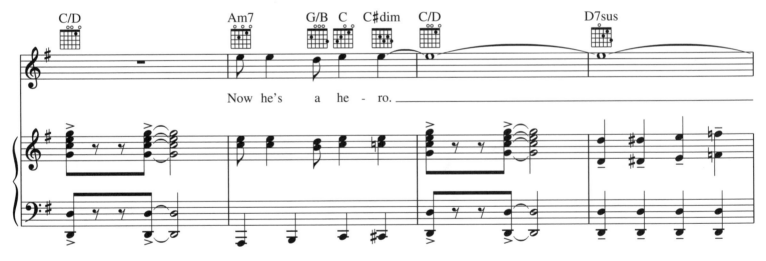

Now he's a he-ro.

Spoken: Yes, in-deed.

Mulan.

MULAN

Music: Matthew Wilder, score by Jerry Goldsmith
Lyrics: David Zippel
Screenplay: Robert D. San Souci based on an
   anonymous poem
Produced by: Pam Coats
Directed by: Barry Cook, Tony Bancroft
Cast: Ming-Na Wen, Lea Salonga (Mulan singing),
   Eddie Murphy, B.D. Wong, Donny Osmond (Shang singing),
   Harvey Fierstein, Jerry S. Tondo, Gedde Watanabe,
   James Hong, Miguel Ferrer, Soon-Tek Oh, Freda Foh Shen,
   Pat Morita, June Foray, George Takei
Songs: "Reflection"; "Honor to Us All"; "I'll Make a Man Out of
   You"; "A Girl Worth Fighting For"; "True to Your Heart"
Released: June 1998; 88 minutes

Disney's thirty-sixth animated full-length film, *Mulan*, like so many of the previous films, centers on a plucky heroine and provides a lovable animal sidekick. The story is taken from an ancient Chinese folk legend. The Emperor decrees that one man from each family must step forward to fight against the Huns. In order to spare her aged, ailing father from the hardships and dangers of war, Mulan steals the family sword, disguises herself as a boy and runs off to join the army. The film balances feminist ideals and romance as Mulan flies in the face of society's conventions and expectations. She is joined in her adventures by a tiny, street-smart dragon named Mushu (Eddie Murphy). Over 700 people were involved in creating the striking animation and artwork. Pop legend Stevie Wonder was brought in to sing "True to Your Heart" over the end credits.

Disney ST. Disney Home Video VC.

Reflection

(Pop Version)

from Walt Disney Pictures' MULAN
As Performed by Christina Aguilera

Music by MATTHEW WILDER
Lyrics by DAVID ZIPPEL

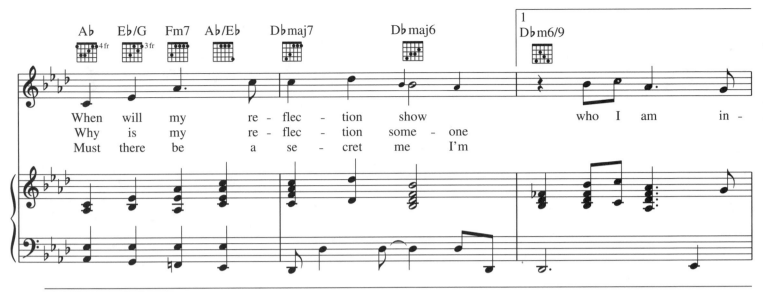

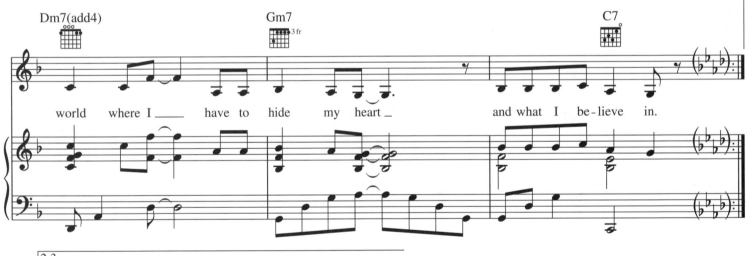

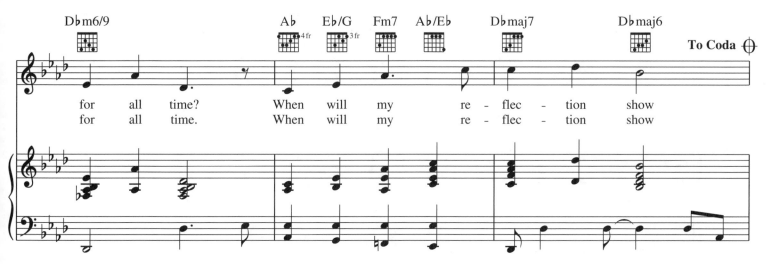

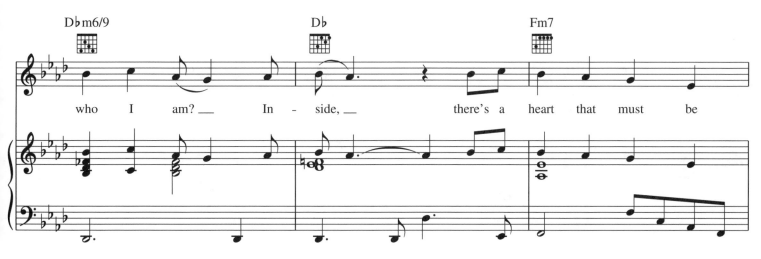

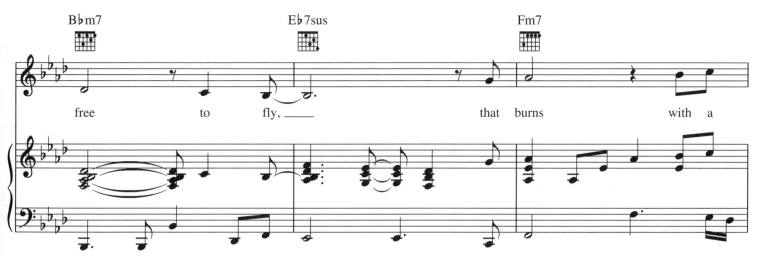

True to Your Heart

(Pop Version)

from Walt Disney Pictures' MULAN

As Recorded by 98 Degrees featuring Stevie Wonder

Music by MATTHEW WILDER
Lyrics by DAVID ZIPPEL

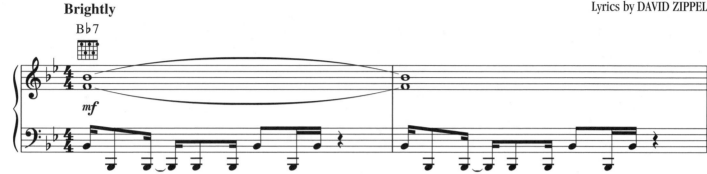

- by, I knew at once __ that you were meant for me. __ Deep __

show - er you with my love. O - pen your eyes, your heart _ can tell _

_ you no lies. And when _ you're true _ to your heart, I know it's

gon - na lead you straight to me. _

(Got _ to be true

to your heart.) _

Some -

F7sus   B7

(Got _ to be   true

to your   heart.) _

Girl, _ my heart _ is driv - ing me _ to where _

_ you are; _   You _ can take both hands off _ the wheel _ and still _

get far. Be _____ swept a - way, _____ en -

joy the ride. _____ You won't __ get lost __ with your

heart to _____ guide you. True __ to your heart, you must __ be true __

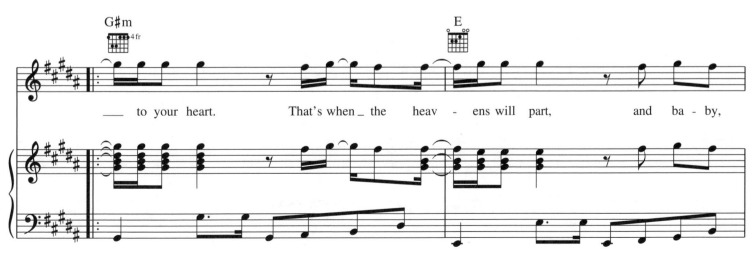

_____ to your heart. That's when __ the heav - ens will part, and ba - by,

show-er you with my love. O - pen your eyes, your heart _ can tell _

_ you no lies. And when _ you're true _ to your heart, I know it's

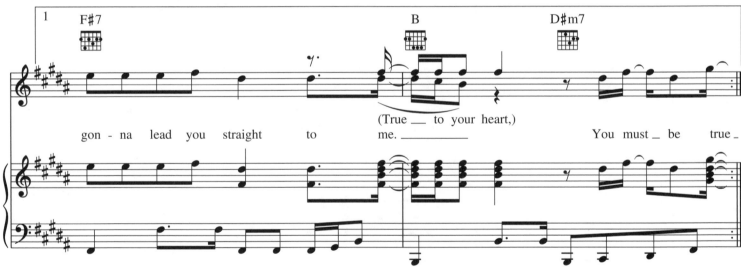

1

(True _ to your heart,)

gon - na lead you straight to me. _____ You must _ be true _

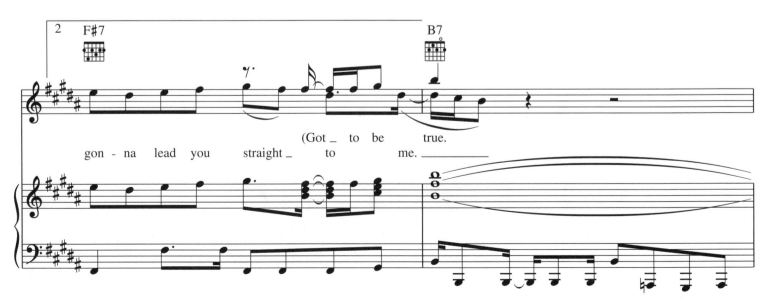

2

(Got _ to be true.

gon - na lead you straight _ to me. _____

to your heart.) __

When things are get - tin' cra - zy
When all the world a - round_ you,

and you don't know where to start, _____ keep on be - liev - in', ba - by;
it __ seems to fall a - part, _____ keep on be - liev - in', ba - by;

just be true __ to your heart.
just be true __ to your heart.

Repeat and Fade

Optional Ending

THE PRINCE OF EGYPT

Music and Lyrics: Stephen Schwartz
Score: Hans Zimmer
Screenplay: Philip LaZebnik, Nicholas Meyer
Produced by: Penney Finkelman Cox, Sandra
   Rabins, Jeffrey Katzenberg (executive producer),
   Ron Rocha (associate producer)
Directed by: Brenda Chapman, Steve Hickner and
   Simon Wells
Voices: Val Kilmer, Ralph Fiennes, Sandra Bullock,
   Helen Mirren, Jeff Goldblum, Michelle Pfeiffer, Patrick Stewart,
   Danny Glover, Martin Short, Steve Martin
Songs: "Deliver Us"; "All I Ever Wanted"; "Through Heaven's Eyes";
   "Playing with the Big Boys"; "The Plagues"; "When You Believe";
   "I Will Get There"
Released: December 1998; 99 minutes

The Prince of Egypt.

With *The Prince of Egypt* DreamWorks Pictures combined two winning Hollywood traditions, a Disney-style animated musical with a Cecille B. DeMille-like Biblical epic story. Stephen Schwartz, successful in his twenties as the composer/lyricist for *Godspell* and *Pippin*, was signed to write the songs. The result is the most serious-minded of animated musicals – despite some added comic characters – and it may have lost some small children in the process. In the familiar story Moses is placed in a basket by his troubled Hebrew slave mother and sent down the Nile, believing that some generous free woman will adopt her infant boy, saving him from Egyptian capture. That someone turns out to be the Queen of Egypt, and Moses is brought up as a prince. Through a happenstance that's part Bible and part Hollywood, Moses encounters his Hebrew siblings, Miriam and Aaron, and learns his true identity. He is greatly changed by the realization, and flees his royal life to find Tzipporah, a Bedouin woman he was once given as a gift but who escaped. The two fall in love and for some years lead a simple life as shepherds. Out of the blue the burning bush appears to him along with the voice of God calling him to return to Egypt and release the Hebrews from their enslavement. He finds that his father has died and his brother, Rameses, has become Pharoah. Moses tries in vain to plead his cause to Rameses, who refuses to comply, even in the face of plagues and widespread famine. Moses warns his brother of one last oncoming plague that God has revealed to him, and again Rameses is deaf to his pleas. After his young son dies, Rameses angrily tells his brother to take the Hebrews and leave Egypt. At the Red Sea the Hebrews encounter the Egyptian army, but God sends a huge fire to block the soldiers. The waters of the Red Sea part, leaving an escape route for Moses and the Hebrews. When the Egyptian army attempts to follow, the waters crash on them, drowning out all danger for the Hebrews. Moses and his people safely travel to a new homeland, and the movie ends with him on Mount Sinai receiving the Ten Commandments. The song "When You Believe" became a hit single in a version by pop divas Whitney Houston and Mariah Carey.

DreamWorks Pictures/DreamWorks Home Entertainment

1998

WHEN YOU BELIEVE

FROM THE PRINCE OF EGYPT

Words and Music by
STEPHEN SCHWARTZ

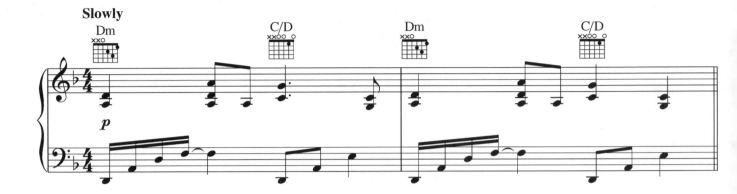

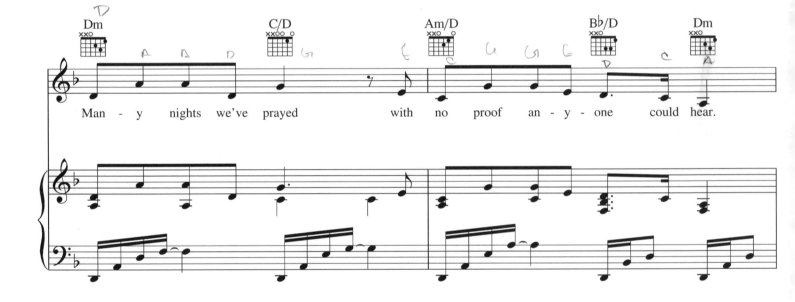

Man - y nights we've prayed with no proof an - y - one could hear.

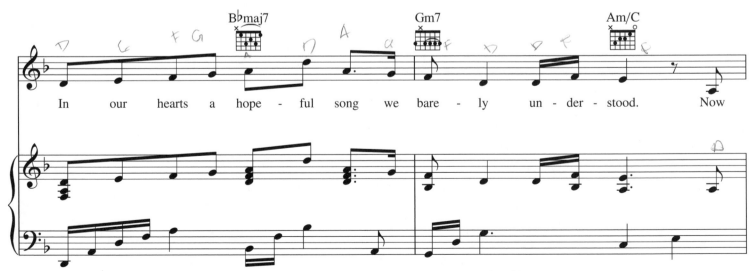

In our hearts a hope - ful song we bare - ly un - der - stood. Now

Original key: E♭ minor. This edition has been transposed down one half-step to be more playable.

how you will, you will when you_____ be - lieve.

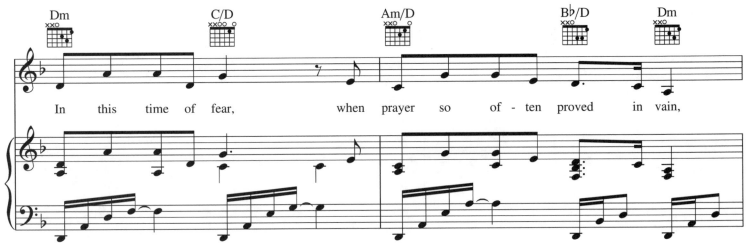

In this time of fear, when prayer so of - ten proved in vain,

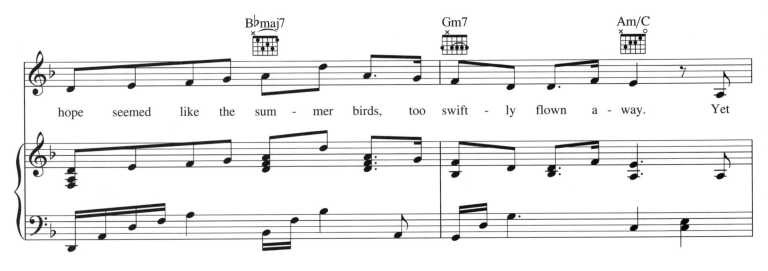

hope seemed like the sum - mer birds, too swift - ly flown a - way. Yet

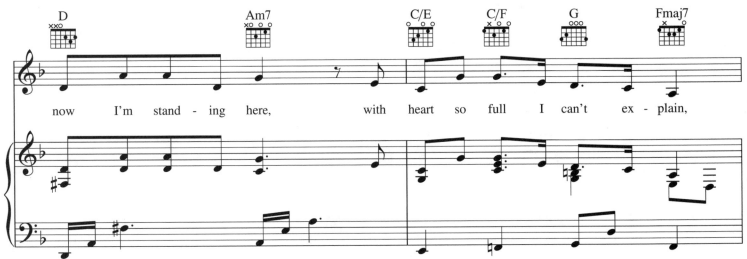

now I'm stand - ing here, with heart so full I can't ex - plain,

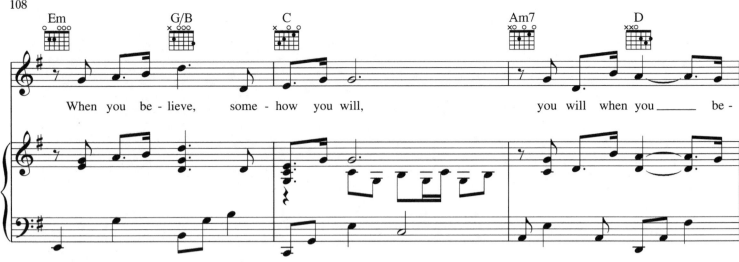

When you be-lieve, some-how you will, you will when you _____ be-

lieve. A-shi-ra _____ l'A-don-ai ki ga-oh ga-ah. A-

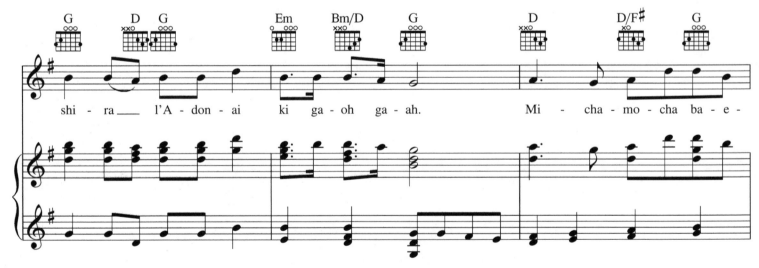

shi-ra _____ l'A-don-ai ki ga-oh ga-ah. Mi-cha-mo-cha ba-e-

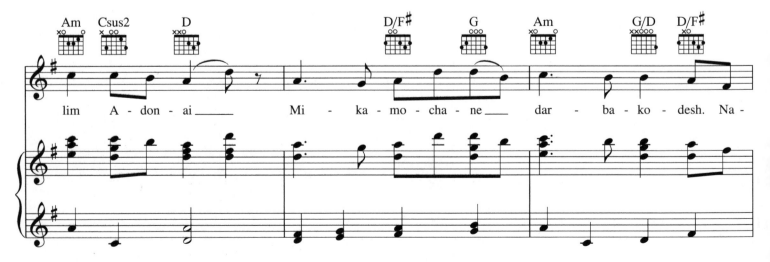

lim A-don-ai _____ Mi-ka-mo-cha-ne _____ dar-ba-ko-desh. Na-

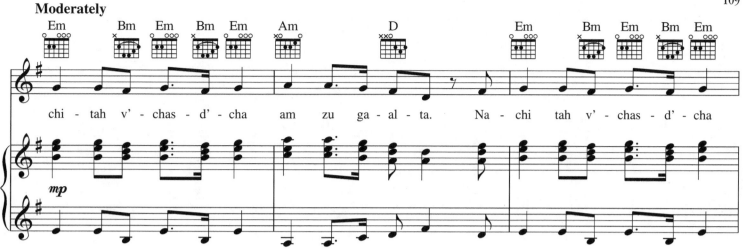

Moderately

chi - tah v'- chas - d' - cha am zu ga - al - ta. Na - chi - tah v'- chas - d' - cha

am zu ga - al - ta. A - shi - ra, a - shi - ra, a - shi - ra. A -

gradual cresc.

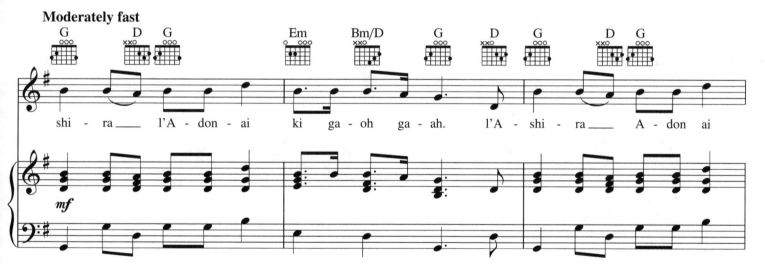

Moderately fast

shi - ra____ l'A - don - ai ki ga - oh ga - ah. l'A - shi - ra____ A - don ai

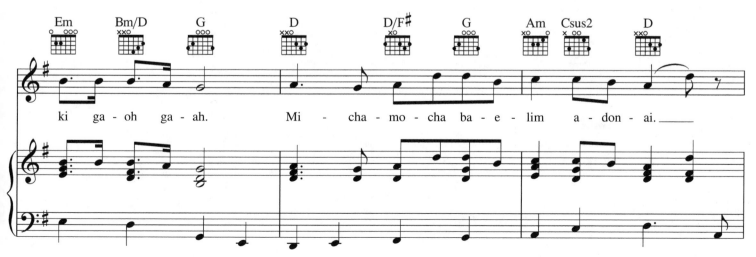

ki ga - oh ga - ah. Mi - cha - mo - cha ba - e - lim a - don - ai.____

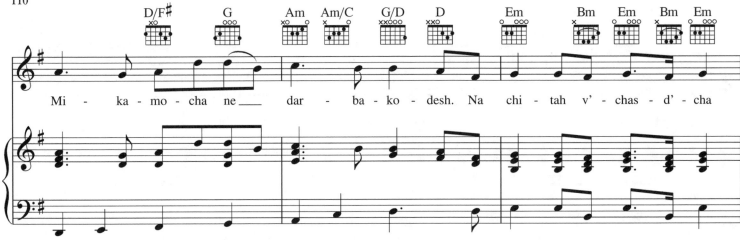

Mi - ka - mo - cha ne___ dar - ba - ko - desh. Na chi - tah v' - chas - d' - cha

am zu ga - al - ta. Na - chi - tah v' - chas - d' - cha am zu ga - al - ta. A -

Moderately slow

shi - ra, a - shi - ra, a - shi - ra. There can be mir - a - cles

when you be - lieve. Though hope is frail, it's hard to kill.

Who knows what mir - a - cles you can a - chieve? When you be - lieve, some -

how you will, now you will. You will when you _____ be -

lieve. You will when you be - lieve. _____

rit.   *sub.* **mp**   *a tempo*

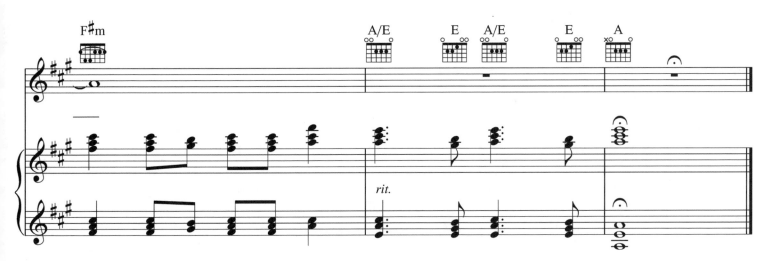

rit.

The Rugrats.

THE RUGRATS MOVIE

Music and Lyrics: Various
Screenplay: David N. Weiss, J. David Stern;
"Rugrats" television series created by
Arlene Klasky, Gabor Csupo, Paul Germain
Produced by: Gabor Csupo and Arlene Klasky for
Klasky-Csupo
Directed by: Norton Virgien and Igor Kovalyov
Voices: David Spade, Whoopi Goldberg, Elizabeth
Daily, Christine Cavanaugh, Kath Souci, Tara Strong, Cheryl
Chase, Melanie Chartoff, Jack Riley, Joe Alaskey, Michael Bell,
Tim Curry, Busta Rhymes, Roger Clinton, Margaret Cho and
others
Songs: "I Throw My Toys Around (Elvis Costello and Cait
O'Riordan); "Take Me There" (Teddy Riley, Tamara Savage,
Mason Betha, Michael Foster); "This World Is Something New
to Me" (Mark Mothersbaugh); "All Day" (Lisa Loeb);
"Dil-A-Bye" (Mark Mothersbaugh); "A Baby Is a Gift from a
Bob" (Mark Mothersbaugh); "One Way or Another"
(Deborah Harry and Nigel Harrison); "Wild Ride" (Mario
Caldato, Jr., Kevin Krakower, Lisa Stone); "On Your Marks,
Get Set, Ready, Go!" (Trevor Smith); "Witch Doctor"
(Ross Bagdasarian); "Take the Train" (Danny Saber,
William Griffin); "Yo Ho Ho and a Bottle of Yum!"
(Mark Mothersbaugh)
Released: November 20, 1998; 79 minutes

L ight on plot and heavy on music of Lou Rawls, Busta Rhymes
and the B-52s, this quirky animated feature is an action-adven-
ture yarn featuring a cast of caricaturized toddlers. The band
of toddlers, made famous via TV's "Nickelodeon," gets loose in
an SUV-like Raptorwagon, in which they lurch from one disaster to
another. The kids' near misses are played out in scenes that take
liberal pokes at the likes of *Indiana Jones, Jurassic Park* and others. Predatory animals, harrowing, cliff-hanging scenes and a train
full of circus monkeys all figure into the story. The scatological
humor, of the sandbox variety, and stream of consciousness dialog
of this film are clearly aimed at children, unlike films of the *Toy
Story* ilk, which play to young and old at once.

Paramount Pictures Nickelodeon Movies Klasky Csupo Inc.

Yo Ho Ho and a Bottle of Yum!

FROM THE PARAMOUNT MOTION PICTURE SOUNDTRACK THE RUGRATS MOVIE

Words and Music by
MARK MOTHERSBAUGH

Brightly

(Spoken:) Love the poop deck, Mr. Phil. Hoist the anchor, Number One. Aye Aye, Cap'n. A

pi-rate's life is a life for me. Yo ho ho and a bot-tle of yum. But I got sea-sick on the sea.

Yo ho ho and a bot-tle of yum. Hoist our Rep-tar flag real high. My sword is point-ed to the sky. You

need a patch a-cross your eye. Yo. Yo. To

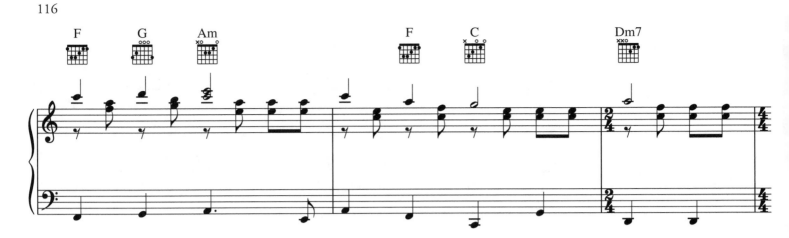

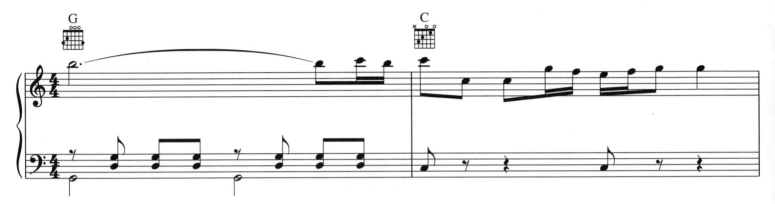

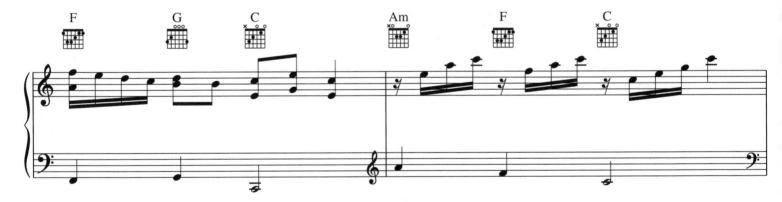

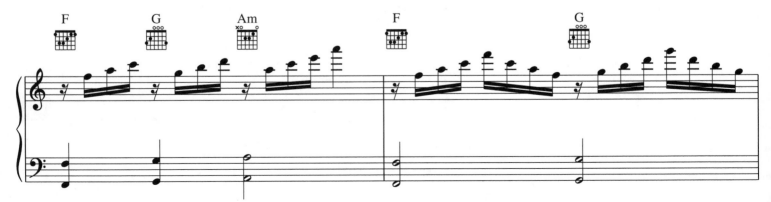

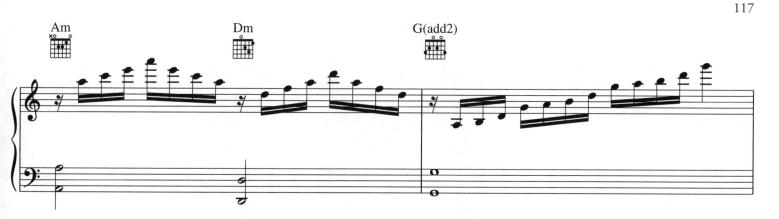

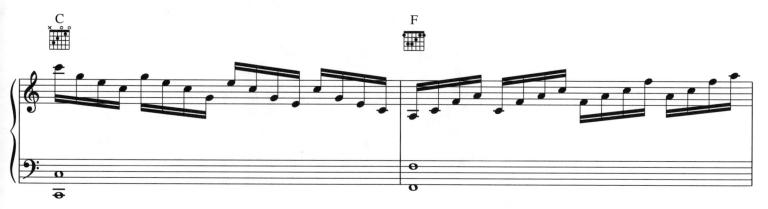

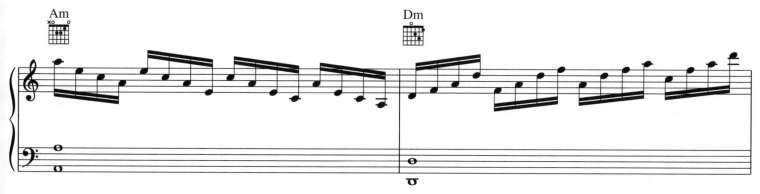

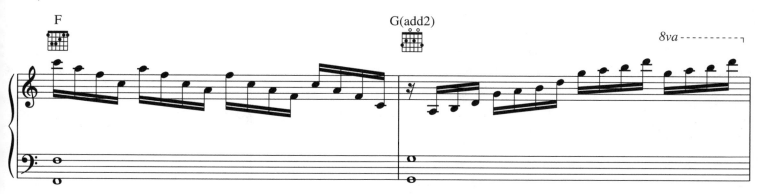

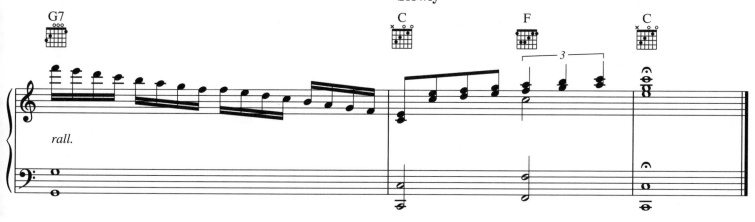

Buena Vista Social Club

Music and Lyrics: Various
Screenplay: Wim Wenders
Produced by: Deepak Nayar and Ulrich Felsberg
   for Road Movies
Directed by: Wim Wenders
Photography: Robby Müller, Lisa Rinzler,
   Jörg Widmer
Cast: Luis Barzaga, Joachim Cooder, Ry Cooder, Julio
   Alberto Fernández, Ibrahim Ferrer, Carlos
   González, Rubén González, Salvador Repilado
   Labrada, Pio Leyva, Manuel "Puntillita" Licea,
   Orlando "Cachaíto" López, Benito Suárez Magana,
   Manuel "Guajiro" Mirabal, Eliades Ochoa, Omara
   Portuondo, Compay Segundo, Julienne Oviedo Sánchez,
   Barbarito Torres, Alberto "Virgilio" Valdés, Amadito Valdés,
   Lázaro Villa, Juan de Marcos González
Songs: "Chan Chan" (Francisco Repilado); "Silencio" (Rafael
   Hernandez); Chattanooga Choo Choo" (Harry Warren and
   Mark Gordon); "Social Club Buena Vista" (Israel López);
   Dos Gardenias"(Isolina Carillo); "Viente Años" (Maria Teresa
   Vera); "Amor de Loca Juventud" (Rafael Ortiz); and others
Released: June 1999; 105 minutes

Ibrahim Ferrer.

Although *Buena Vista Social Club* took fairly harsh criticism
for its production values and editing, the documentary introduced the world to a forgotten era in Cuba's rich musical
past. The film's subjects are the elderly musicians who were
once the lifeblood of Havana's hot musical scene. But Cuba under
Castro had no room for a musical scene. The musicians were
forced to find other livelihoods, and Havana's days of cosmopolitan
glory were gradually forgotten. The film, shot with shaky cameras
in the decaying Havana vestiges of that lost era, allows these musicians to tell their own stories. The stories are often inserted into
musical numbers leaving one hungry for an uninterrupted tune.
The film follows the musicians to New York for a Carnegie Hall
concert and likewise to Amsterdam. If the film, which received an
Academy Award nomination for Best Documentary in 2000, is
more about the stories than the music, the 1997 Grammy-award-
winning album is all about the music.

Sony Road Movies Artisan

Amor de Loca Juventud

from Buena Vista Social Club

Words and Music by
RAFAEL ORTIZ

Bright Gospel Blues

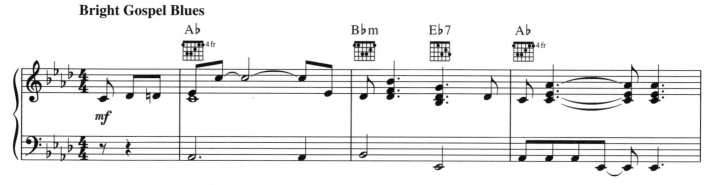

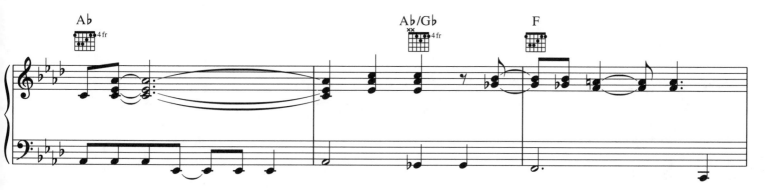

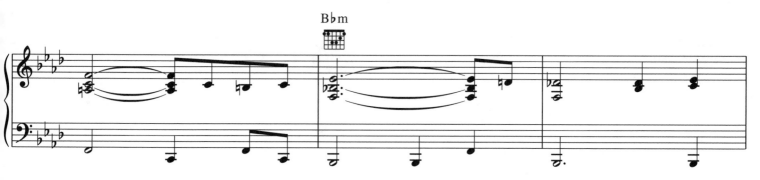

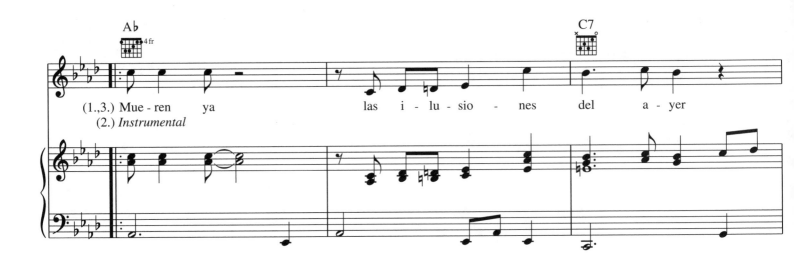

(1.,3.) Mue - ren ya las i - lu - sio - nes del a - yer

(2.) *Instrumental*

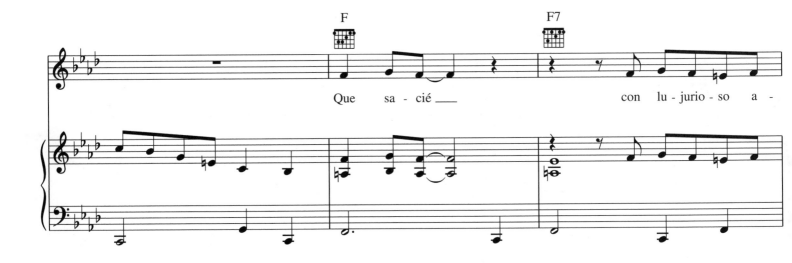

Que sa - cié ___ con lu - jurio - so a -

mor

Y mue - re tam - bién ___

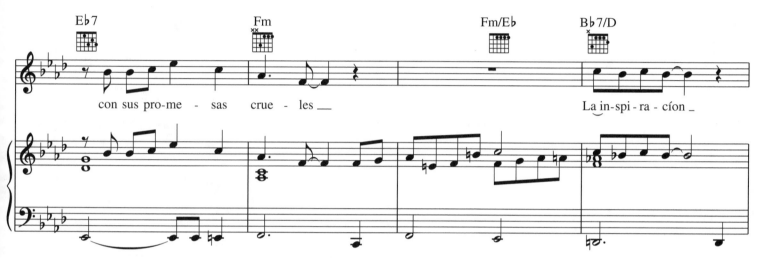

con sus pro - me - sas crue - les ___

La in - spi - ra - cíon ___

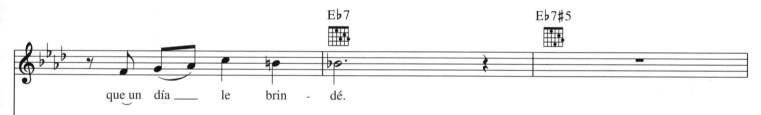

que un día ___ le brin - dé.

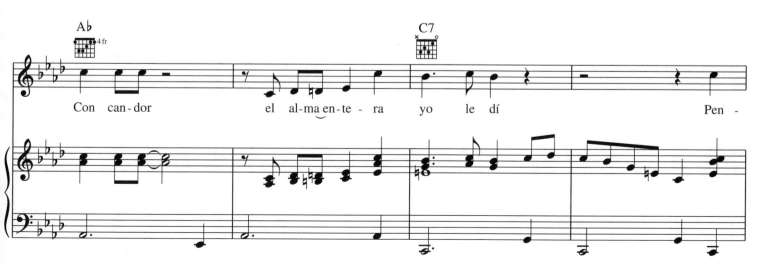

Con can - dor el al - ma en - te - ra yo le dí

Pen -

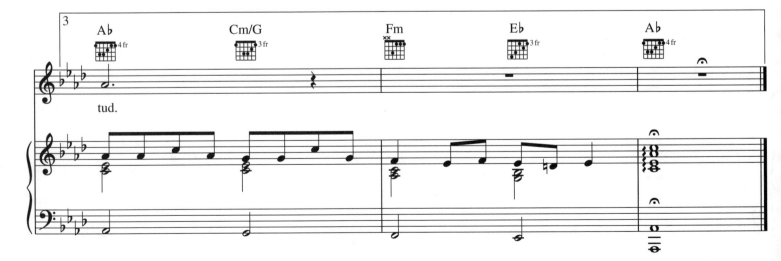

san - do __ nues - tro i - di - lio con - sa - grar

Sin pen - sar que e-lla lo que bus - ca - ba en mí

E-ra el a - mor _ de lo-ca ju-ven - tud.

tud.

Social Club Buena Vista

from Buena Vista Social Club

Words and Music by
ISRAEL LOPEZ

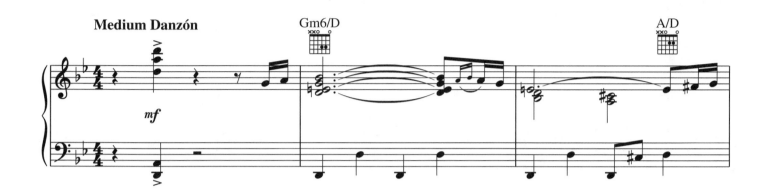

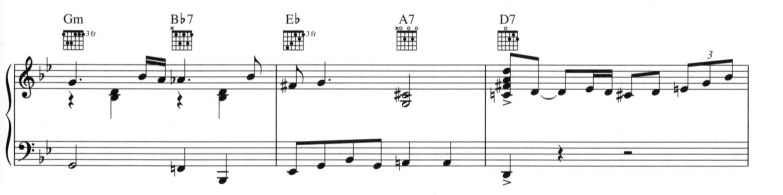

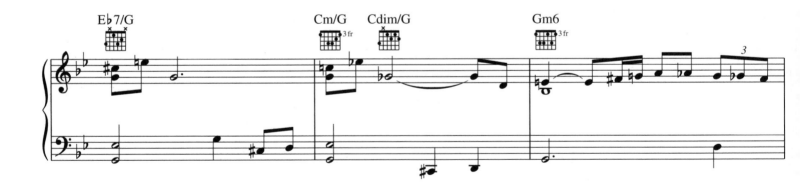

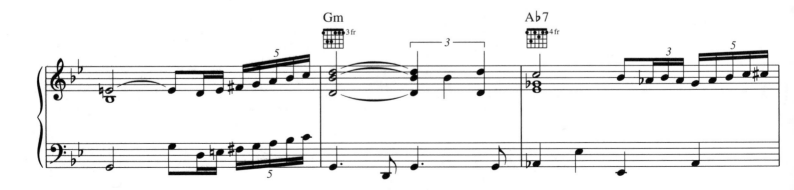

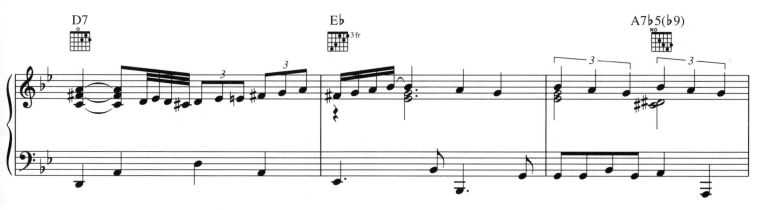

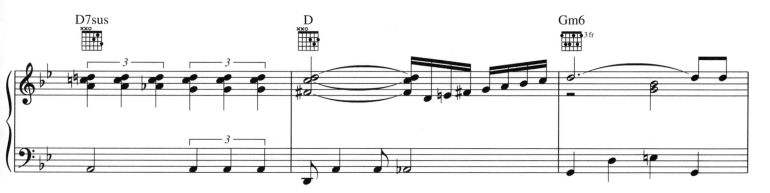

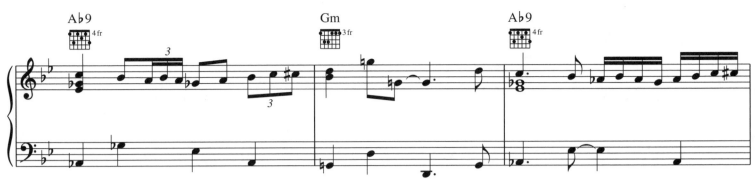

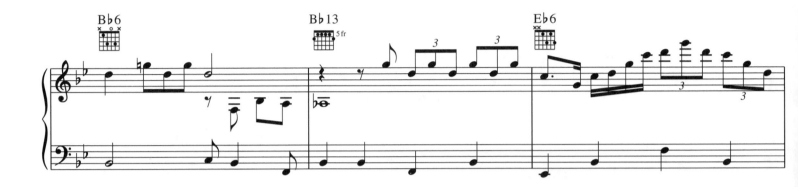

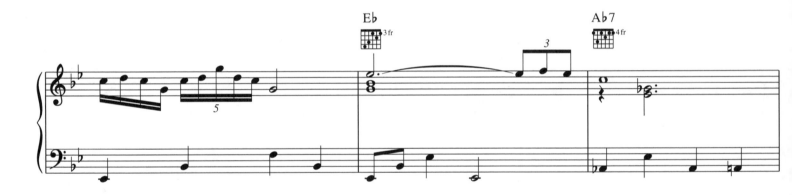

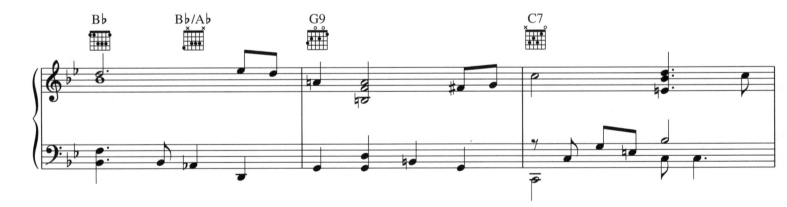

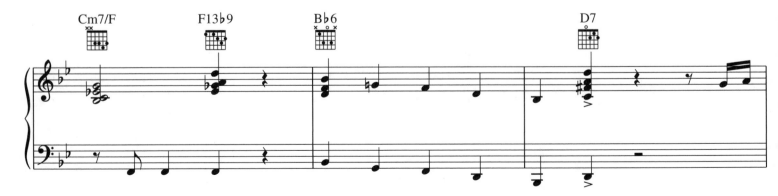

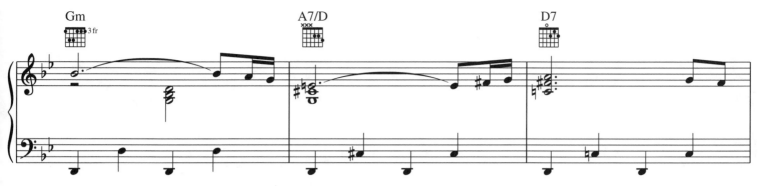

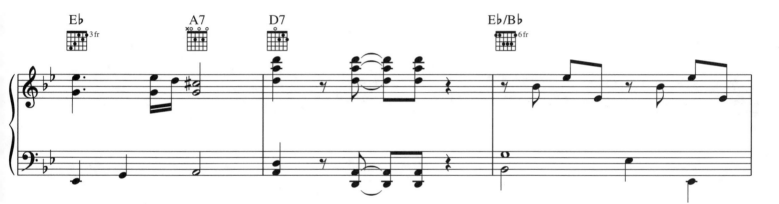

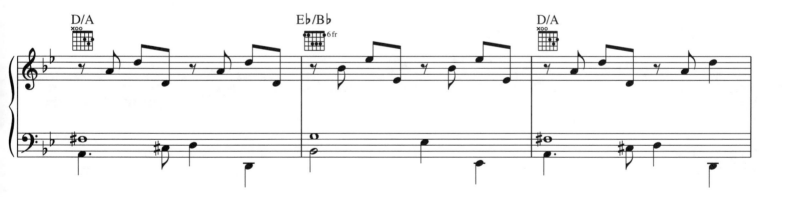

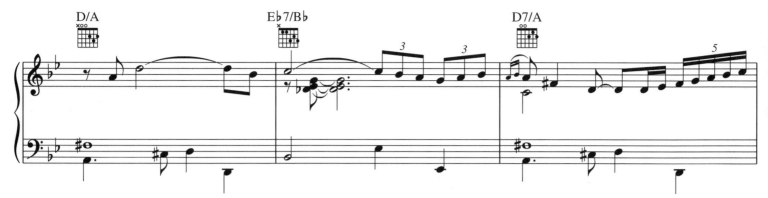

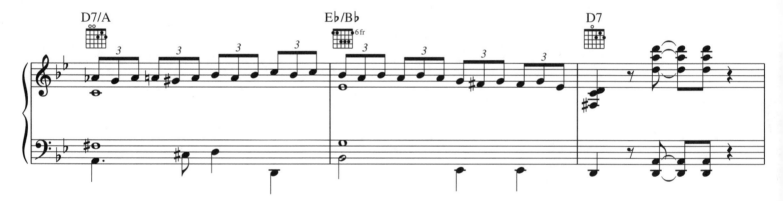

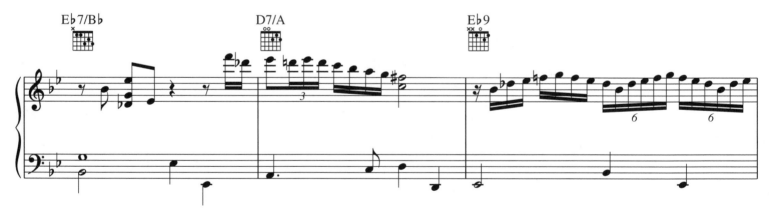

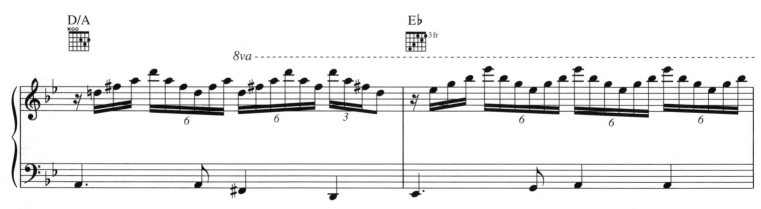

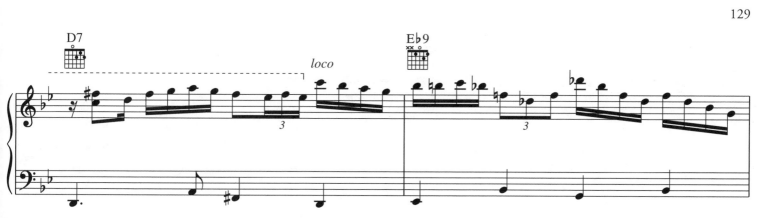

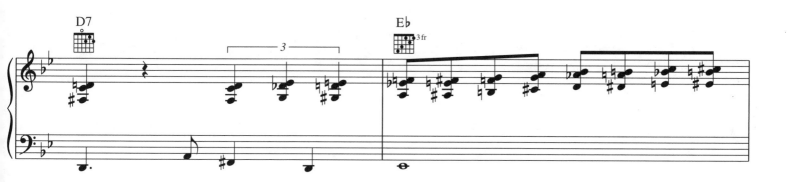

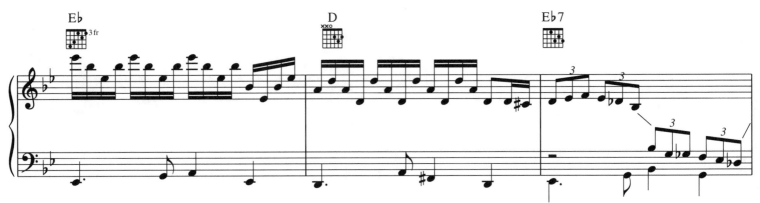

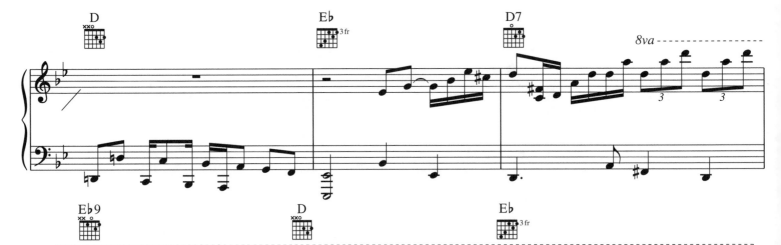

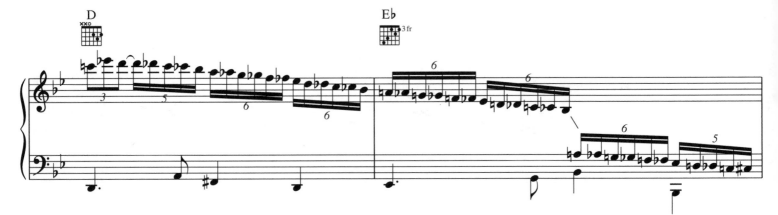

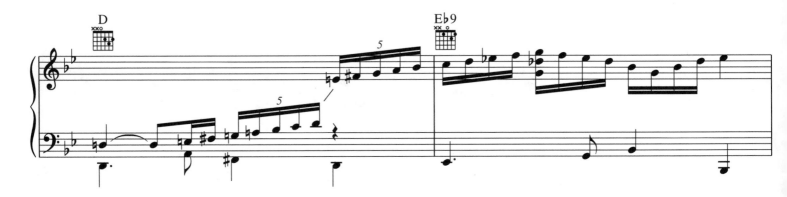

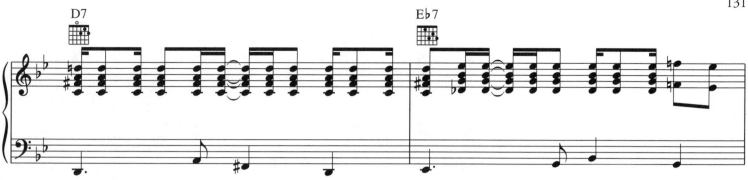

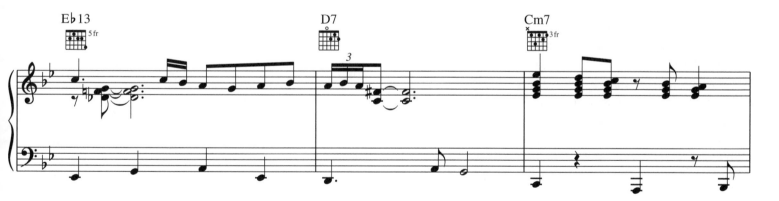

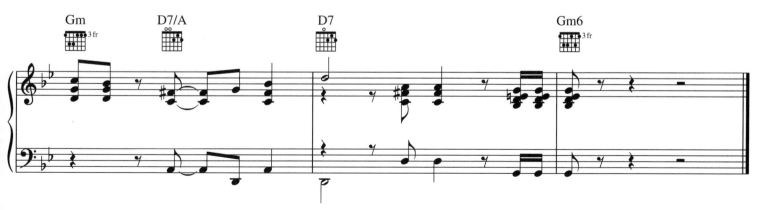

Tarzan™

Music and Lyrics: Phil Collins
Screenplay: Tab Murphy, adapted from the novel
    by Edgar Rice Burroughs
Directed by: Chris Buck, Kevin Lima
Voices: Tony Goldwyn, Wayne Knight, Brian Blessed,
    Nigel Hawthorne, Glenn Close, Minnie Driver,
    Lance Henriksen, Rosie O'Donnell
Songs: "Son of Man"; "Strangers Like Me";
    "Trashin' the Camp"; "Two Worlds";
    "You'll Be in My Heart"
Released: June 1999; 88 minutes

Professor Archimedes Q. Porter, Jane Porter and Tarzan.

Tarzan and Hollywood. The tradition of film renderings of Edgar Rice Burroughs's famous jungle character, first introduced in the 1912 novel *Tarzan of the Apes*, goes back to the silent era. Besides over two dozen novels, many comic books, and radio and television programs, there have been 43 film adaptations of *Tarzan* in various guises. The story is basic, familiar to everyone who has seen the timeless films of the 1930s starring Johnny Weismuller and Maureen O'Hara. Tarzan is an orphan boy, left in the African jungle, adopted by a gorilla family. He grows up happy and unselfconscious, until one day a human expedition intrudes, including a zoologist, Professor Porter, his beautiful daughter Jane, and their greedy jungle guide, Clayton. Tarzan learns his true nature when he meets the humans, and is torn by where his allegiance should lie. This is complicated by falling in love with Jane. Through the villianous Clayton the humans show their mean side, threatening the apes with capture. Tarzan instinctively defends his ape family, pledging his loyalty to them. Jane stays in the jungle with him, of course. Unlike other Disney musicals, most of the songs are sung by Phil Collins on the soundtrack, rather than emanating from the characters themselves, and become like animated MTV music video numbers. Disney's animators continued to push the technological envelope in *Tarzan*, employing the computer-generated illusion of a three-dimensional background.

Walt Disney Pictures/Walt Disney Home Video

Two Worlds

from Walt Disney Pictures' Tarzan ™

Words and Music by
PHIL COLLINS

Moderately

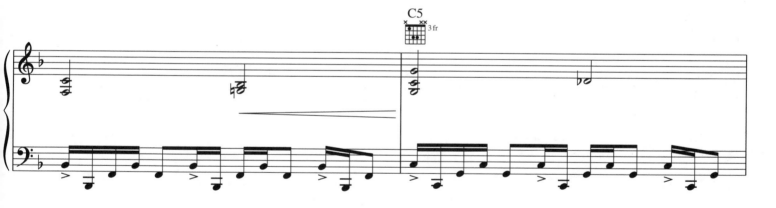

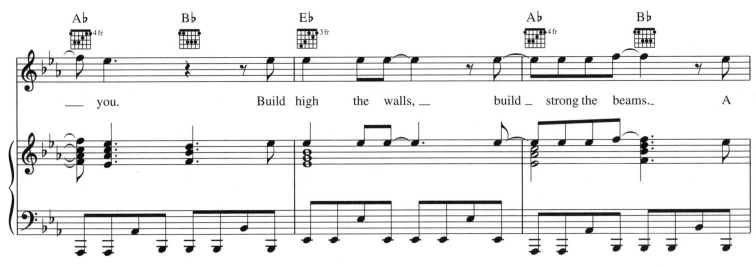

you. Build high the walls, _ build _ strong the beams._ A

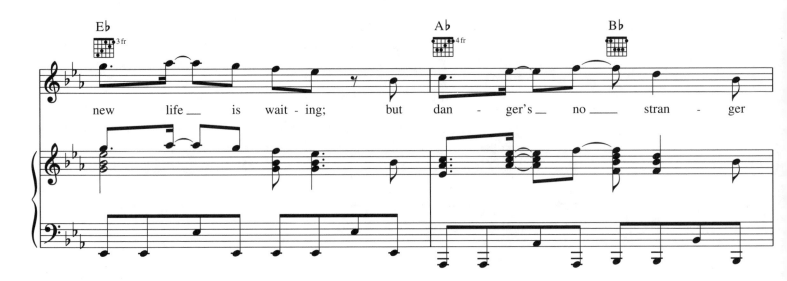

new life _ is wait - ing; but dan - ger's _ no _ stran - ger

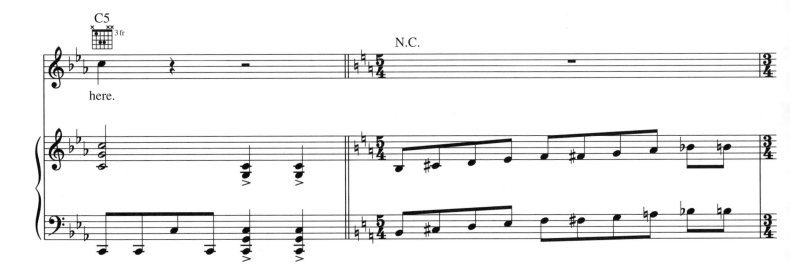

here.

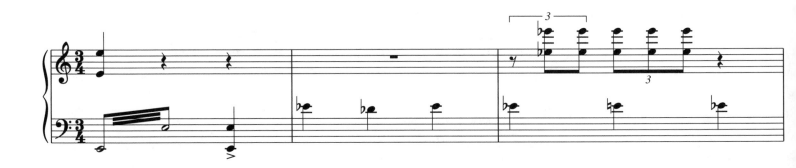

No words de - scribe__ a

moth-er's tears.   No words can__ heal a bro -

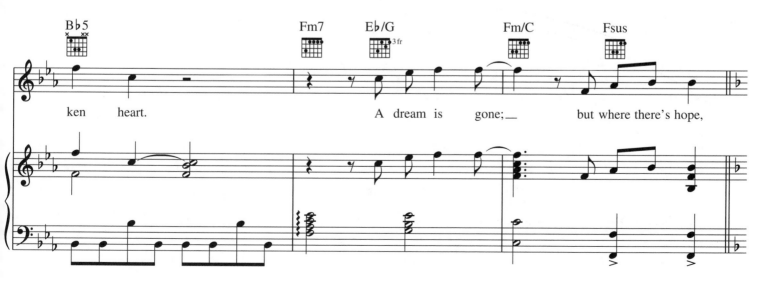

ken heart.   A dream is gone;__ but where there's hope,

some-where,_ some-thing is call - ing__ for__ you. Two worlds,_ one

fam - i - ly. __ Trust your_ heart,_ let fate de - cide_ to

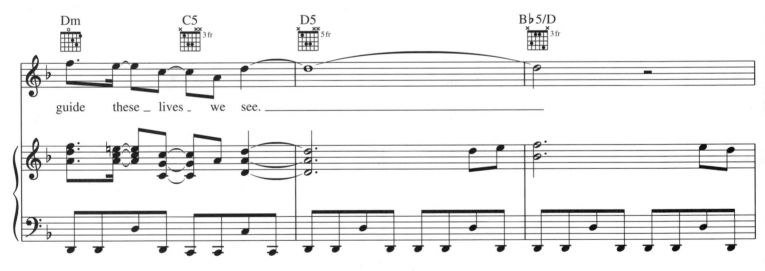

guide these _ lives _ we see. _____

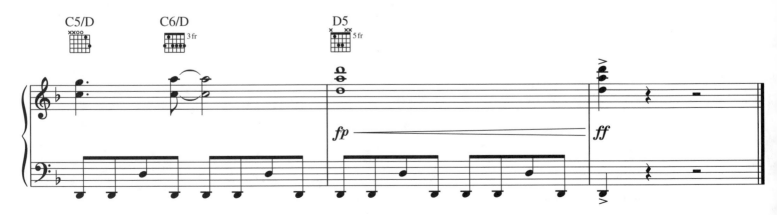

You'll Be in My Heart

(Pop Version)

from Walt Disney Pictures' TARZAN ™

As Performed by Phil Collins

Words and Music by
PHIL COLLINS

Come stop your cry - ing; it will be all right.

Just take my hand, hold it tight. I will pro - tect you from

all a - round you. I will be here; don't you cry.

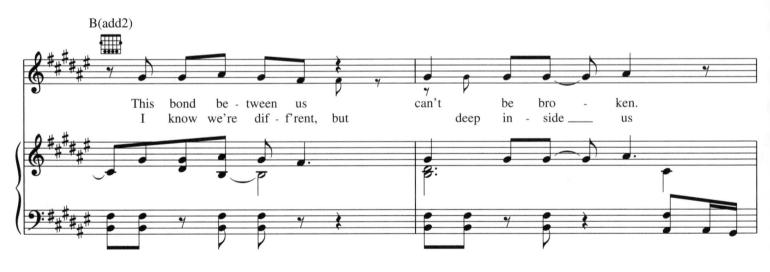

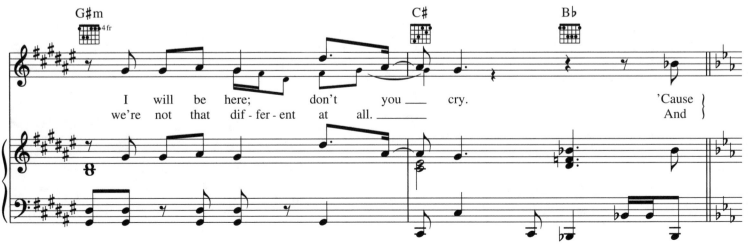

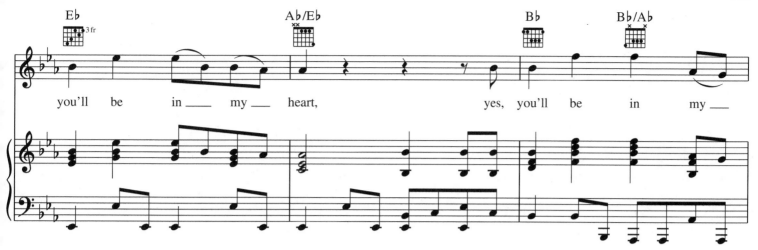

you'll be in __ my __ heart, yes, you'll be in my __

heart from this day on __ now __ and for - ev - er -

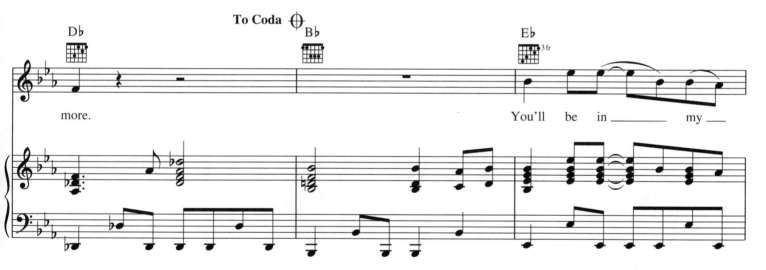

To Coda ⊕

more. You'll be in __ my __

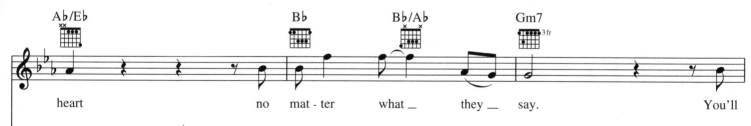

heart no mat - ter what __ they __ say. You'll

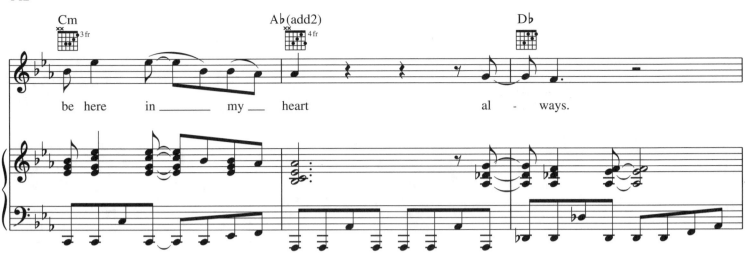

be here in ____ my ___ heart al - ways.

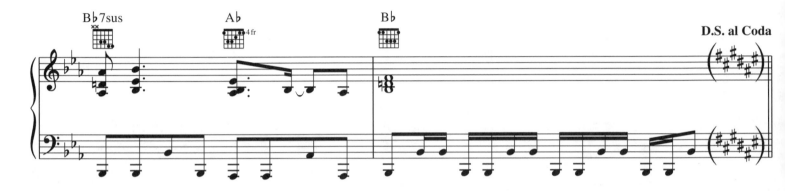

D.S. al Coda

CODA

Don't lis - ten to them, ____ 'cause
des - ti - ny calls__ you you

what do they ___ know?___ We need each oth - er to
must ___ be ___ strong. ___ It may not be with you, but you've

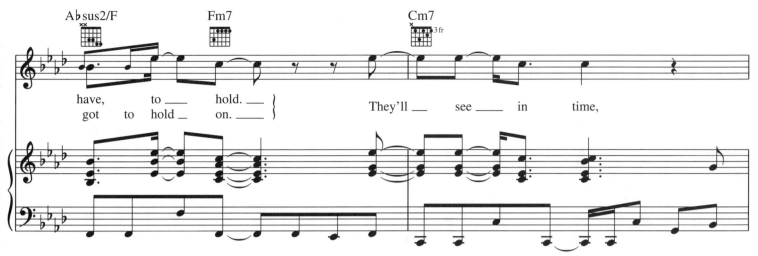

have, to ___ hold. ___
got to hold ___ on. ___

They'll ___ see ___ in time,

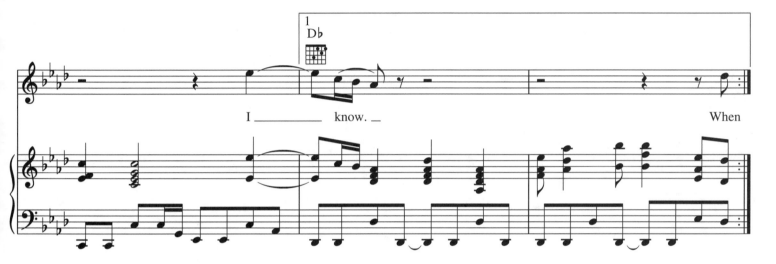

I _____ know. ___

When

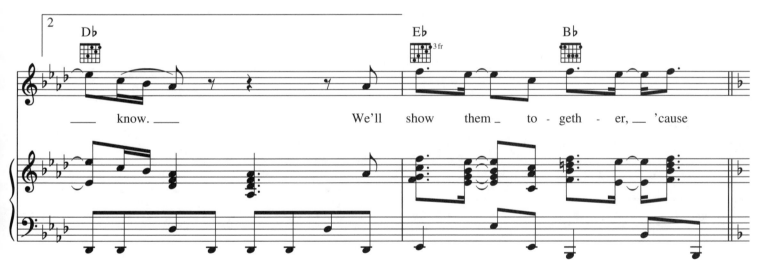

___ know. ___

We'll show them ___ to - geth - er, ___ 'cause

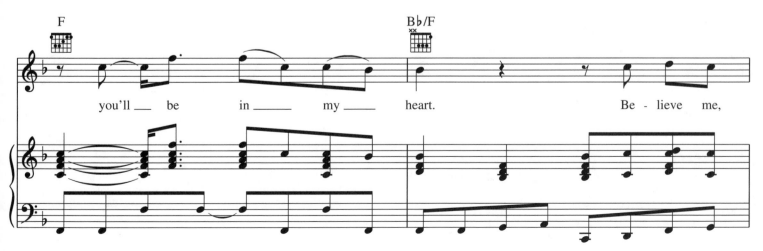

you'll ___ be in _____ my ___ heart.

Be - lieve me,

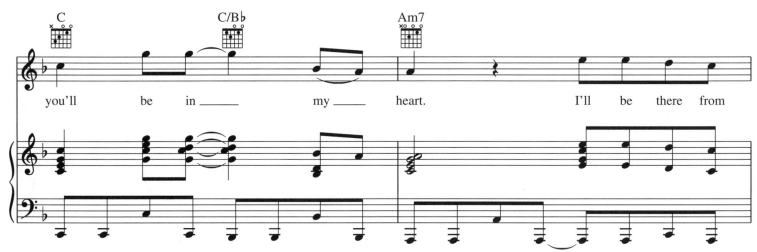

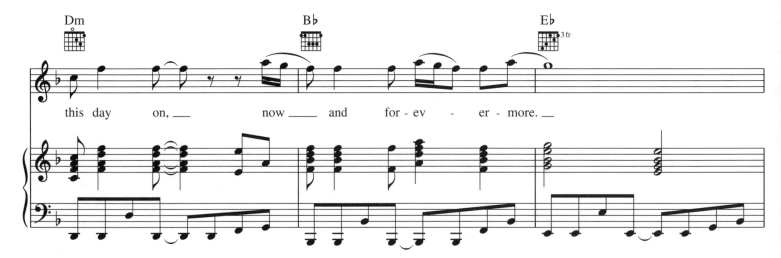

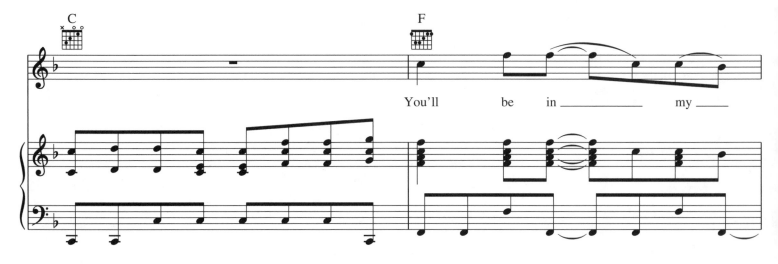

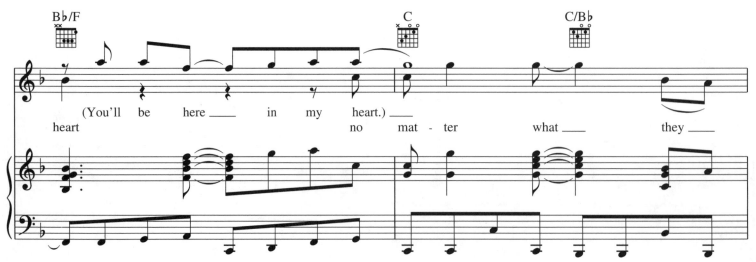

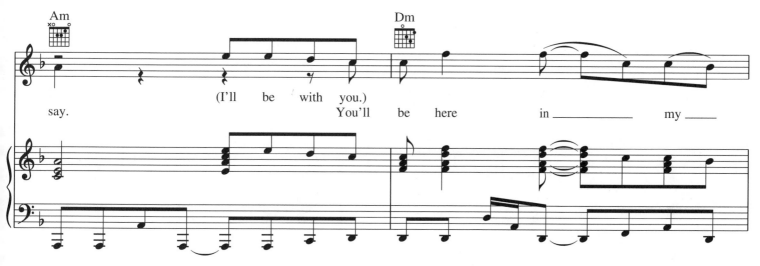

(I'll be with you.)
say. You'll be here in _____ my ____

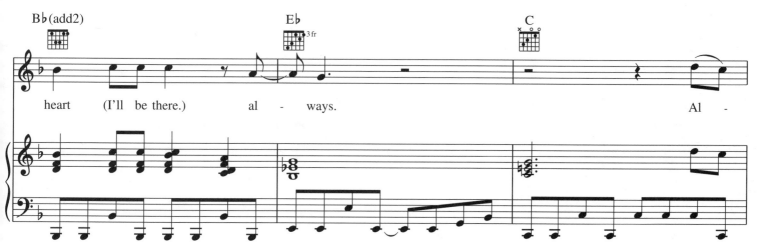

heart (I'll be there.) al - ways. Al -

ways _____ I'll be with you.

I'll be there for __ you al - ways,

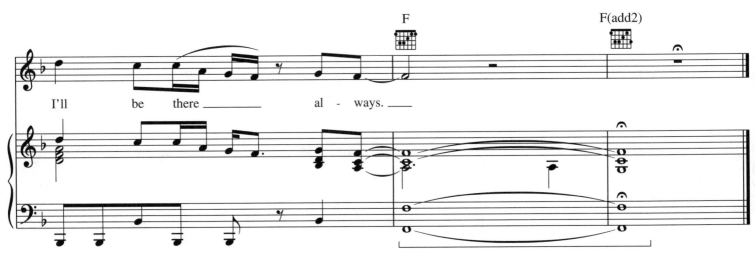

Toy Story 2

Music and Lyrics: Randy Newman
Screenplay: Andrew Stanton, Rita Hsiao, Doug
    Chamberlian and Chris Webb; on an original story
    by John Lasseter, Peter Doctor, Ash Brannon and
    Andrew Stanton
Produced by: Karen Robert Jackson and
    Helene Plotkin
Cinematography by: Sharon Calahan
Directed by: John Lasseter, Lee Unkrich and
    Ash Brannon (Technicolor)
Voices: Tom Hanks, Tim Allen, Joan Cusack, Kelsey Grammer,
    Don Rickles, Jim Varney, Wallace Shawn, John Ratzenberger,
    Annie Potts, Wayne Knight, John Morris, Laurie Metcalf,
    Estelle Harris, R. Lee Ermey and others
Songs: "Woody's Roundup"; "When She Loved Me"
    (Academy Award nomination for Best Song 2000);
    "You've Got a Friend in Me"
Released: November 19, 1999; 92 minutes

Jessie, Buzz Lightyear and Woody.

Toy Story 2 picks up seamlessly where the first film left off. Woody (Tom Hanks), Buzz Lightyear (Tim Allen) and the rest of Andy's toy box gang are back in another death-defying adventure. Woody bravely rescues little Wheezy from the 25-cent bin of a yard sale, only to be kidnapped himself by a fiendish toy store owner (Wayne Knight). The toy store owner needs a Woody doll to make a complete set of the four dolls that were once merchandising for a popular television series, hoping to make a small fortune by selling the set to a toy museum in Japan. Woody, who never knew about his television roots and merchandising fame, is seduced by the permanent glory of a museum collection. Buzz and company arrive to rescue Woody, after a requisite series of adventures including a second Buzz character thrown into the fray, but Woody sends them away. At the last moment he realizes that his friends mean more to him than fame and tries to return with Buzz and the gang. But the museum-bound toys know that without Woody they will go back into storage. Stinky Pete (Kelsey Grammer) forces Woody to stay with the set of dolls bound for Japan. More animated heroics rescue Woody and two of his companions, sending Stinky Pete off to live with a child. Like the original Toy Story, this is a film for anyone who has ever had a toy.

Walt Disney Pictures Pixar Animation Studios

When She Loved Me

FROM WALT DISNEY PICTURES' TOY STORY 2 - A PIXAR FILM

Music and Lyrics by
RANDY NEWMAN

When some - bod-y loved me, ev - 'ry-thing was beau-ti-ful.

Ev - 'ry hour we spent to-geth - er lives with-in my heart. And when she was sad,

I was there to dry her tears; and when she was hap-py, so ___ was I, when

The Emperor's New Groove.

THE EMPEROR'S NEW GROOVE

Music: Sting and David Hartley

Lyrics: Sting

Score: John Debney

Screenplay: David Reynolds, based on a story by Roger Allers, Chris Williams, Mark Dindal and Matthew Jacob

Produced by: Randy Fullmer for Walt Disney Productions

Directed by: Mark Dindal (Technicolor)

Voices: David Spade, John Goodman, Eartha Kitt, Patrick Warburton, Wendie Malick

Songs: "Perfect World"; "My Funny Friend and Me" (Academy Award nomination for Best Song 2001); "Snuff Out the Lights"; "Walk the Llama Llama"; "One Day She'll Love Me"

Released: December 15, 2000; 78 minutes

The Emperor's New Groove is not an epic tale set to sweeping music, as are so many of the Disney animated features. It is a goofy, slap-stick story told with the stand-up wit of prime time television. David Spade is heard as the whiny, self-obsessed Emperor Kuzco. When Kuzco fires his assistant Yzma, a "wicked witch" character read by Eartha Kitt, he sets himself up for disaster. Yzma enlists the help of Kronk (Patrick Warburton), a hulking chef who has neither heart nor stomach for evil deeds, to poison the Emperor. But the poison fails to kill him, turning him into a llama instead. A kindly character named Pacha (John Goodman) finds Emperor/llama Kuzco and helps him regain the throne, even though he knows that Kuzco will destroy his village to make way for a resort once he is back in power. This film is entertainment in the style of Saturday morning cartoons.

Walt Disney Pictures/Walt Disney Home Video

2000

My Funny Friend and Me

FROM WALT DISNEY PICTURES' THE EMPEROR'S NEW GROOVE

Lyrics by STING
Music by STING and DAVID HARTLEY

In the qui - et time of eve - ning, when the stars as-sume their

pat - terns __ and the day has made his jour - ney,

and we won-der just what hap-pened to the life we knew, be-fore the world changed, when not a

Fantasia 2000.

Fantasia 2000

Music: various

Screenplay: Carl Fallberg, Irene Mecchi, Perce Pearce, David Reynolds; with a story by Hans Christian Andersen

Produced by: Donald W. Ernst for Walt Disney Productions

Directed by: James Algar, Gaëtan Brizzi and others

Cast: Steve Martin, Itzhak Perlman, Quincy Jones, Bette Midler, James Earl Jones, Penn & Teller, James Levine, Angela Lansbury

Musical selections: "Symphony No. 5" (Beethoven); "Pines of Rome" (Respighi); "Rhapsody in Blue" (Gershwin); "Piano Concerto No. 2, Allegro" (Shostakovich); "Carnival of the Animals" finale (Saint Saëns); "The Sorcerer's Apprentice" (Dukas); "Pomp and Circumstance – Marches 1,2,3, and 4" (Elgar); "Firebird Suite" (Stravinsky – 1919 version)

Released: December 1999; 75 minutes

Walt Disney's 1940 *Fantasia* was intended to be an ongoing, ever-changing work of art. Disney intended to add and remove segments over the years, so that it would continue to be a fresh experience for audiences. The 1940 *Fantasia* called for theater owners to install 64 speakers so that audiences would get an overwhelming sonic experience. Few, if any, theaters came up with the required speakers. The country was too intent on watching World War II develop to take much notice of the fanciful Disney release at the time. A revival of the film in 1968 found a new audience seeking a "mind-expanding" experience. But Walt Disney's vision for the animated film was not realized until the release of *Fantasia 2000*, designed for the mammoth speaker systems and five-story screens of IMAX theaters. Like the original, *Fantasia 2000* depicts "the kind of images that might pass through your mind as you sit in a concert hall listening to music." All that remains of the original film is the much-loved "The Sorcerer's Apprentice" segment. Animation and recording technology have grown up in the 60 years since *Fantasia* first appeared, and this film takes full advantage of both.

Walt Disney Pictures Walt Disney Home Video

CARNIVAL OF THE ANIMALS

FROM WALT DISNEY PICTURES' FANTASIA 2000

By CAMILLE SAINT-SAËNS

Molto allegro

Miguel and Tulio.

THE ROAD TO EL DORADO

Music: Elton John
Lyrics: Tim Rice
Score: Hans Zimmer and John Powell
Screenplay: Ted Elliot, Terry Rossio
Produced by: Bonne Radford, Brooke Breton for
　DreamWorks
Directed by: Eric "Bibo" Bergeron,
　Don Paul (Technicolor)
Voices: Kevin Kline, Kenneth Branagh, Rosie Perez, Armand
　Assante, Edward James Olmos, Jim Cummings, Frank Welker,
　Elton John (narrator), and others
Songs: "El Dorado"; The Trail We Blaze"; It's Tough to Be a
　God"; "Without Question"; "Friends Never Say Goodbye";
　"Someday Out of the Blue (Theme from El Dorado)";
　"Wonders of the New World: To Shibalba"
Released: March 31, 2000; 89 minutes

Competing with the wildly successful animated features of
Disney is no small task. This DreamWorks entry into the
Disney-dominated genre is a light-hearted romp complete
with love interest, evil fiend and obligatory moral. The plot
features two good-natured, wisecracking friends, Tulio (Kevin
Kline) and Miguel (Kenneth Branagh) who get in above their
heads thanks to a treasure map and a high seas escape in a row
boat—with a horse. When they finally wash up on an island, it
turns out to be just where the map was leading them. Treasure and
riches abound with just one hitch—the locals think they are gods.
The only locals not convinced of their lofty status are Chel (Rosie
Perez) a sort of street-smart serving girl, and Tzekel-Kan (Armand
Assante), an evil, power-hungry priest. A solid story, the movie
rides on the jovial interplay between Kline and Branagh, whose
animated characters resemble the two actors.

DreamWorks Pictures/DreamWorks Home Entertainment

2000

Someday Out of the Blue
(Theme from El Dorado)
from The Road to El Dorado

Music by ELTON JOHN and PATRICK LEONARD
Lyrics by TIM RICE

*Guitarists: Slide capo to 4th fret.

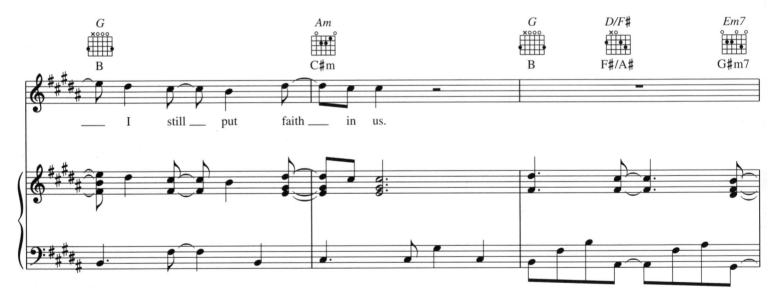

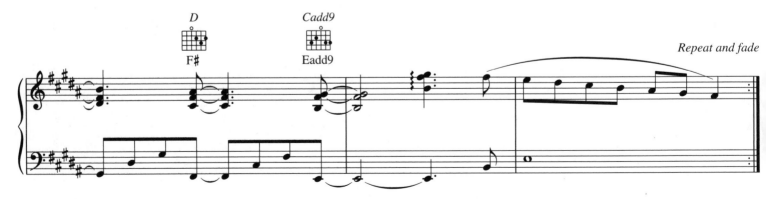

Friends Never Say Goodbye

FROM THE ROAD TO EL DORADO

Music by ELTON JOHN
Lyrics by TIM RICE

The Tigger Movie

Music and Lyrics: Richard M. Sherman and Robert B. Sherman (with Kenny Loggins on "Your Heart Will Lead You Home")

Score: Harry Gregson-Williams

Screenplay: Jun Falkenstein on characters by A.A. Milne and story by Eddie Guzelian

Produced by: Cheryl Abood for Walt Disney Animation

Directed by: Jun Falkenstein (Technicolor)

Voices: Jim Cummings, Nikita Hopkins, Ken Sansom, John Fiedler, Peter Cullen, Andre Stojka, Kath Souci, Tom Attenborough, John Hurt, Frank Welker

Songs: "The Wonderful Thing About Tiggers"; "Someone Like Me"; "Whoop-De-Dooper Bounce"; "Pooh's Lullabee"; "Round My Family Tree"; "How to Be a Tigger"; "Your Heart Will Lead You Home"

Released: February 11, 2000; 77 minutes

The Tigger Movie.

This is a gentle-spirited children's film, told by the lovable characters of A.A. Milne's *Winnie-the-Pooh*. The familiar characters are portrayed by wonderfully unique caricature voices that define and identify their characters immediately. The characters come to life with quirks, including the irrepressible Tigger's gift for malapropisms. With the exception of a vivid dream scene, the sets and characters are drawn in Milne's soft-hued, watercolor style. The result is a journey into the familiar world of Pooh, Christopher Robin and company.

Walt Disney Home Video

2000

Your Heart Will Lead You Home

FROM WALT DISNEY PICTURES' THE TIGGER MOVIE

Words and Music by RICHARD M. SHERMAN,
ROBERT B. SHERMAN and KENNY LOGGINS

Lyrics:

Sun-ny days and star-ry nights and la-zy af-ter-noons; you're count-ing cas-tles in the clouds and hum-ming lit-tle tunes. But some-how, right be-fore your eyes the sum-mer fades a-way; ev-'ry-thing's

Original key: Db major. This edition has been transposed up one half-step to be more playable.

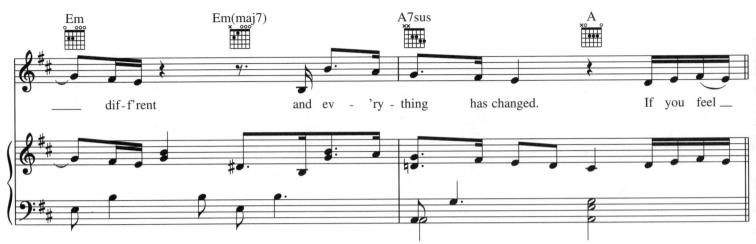

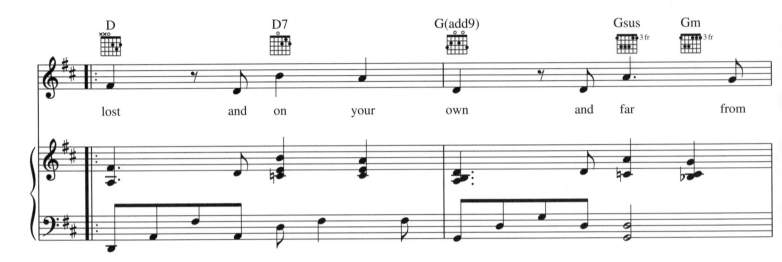

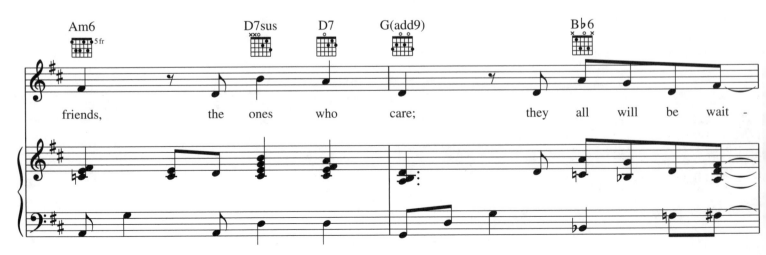

-ing ___ there ___ with love to share ___ and your

heart will lead _____ you home.

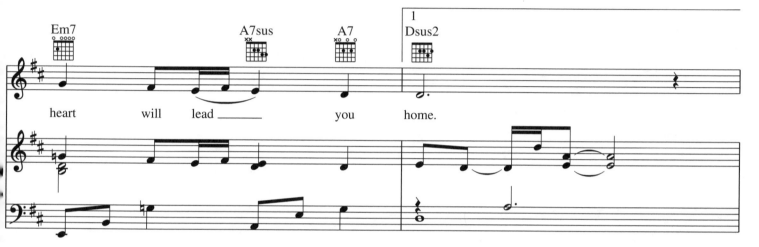

Fun-ny how a pho-to-graph can

take you ___ back in time ___ to plac-es and ___ em-brac-es that you thought ___

__ you'd left be - hind. ___ They're try - ing to __ re - mind __ you that you're not __

___ the on - ly one ___ that no one is an is - land when all is

said and done. _____ If you feel __ home.

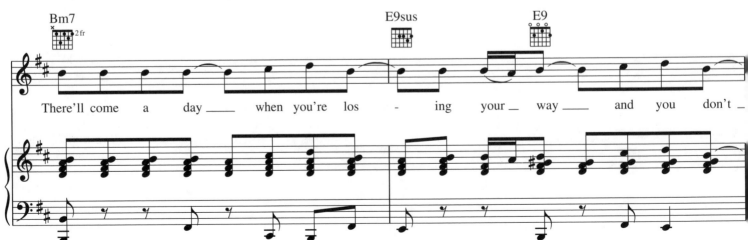

There'll come a day ___ when you're los - ing your __ way ___ and you don't __

home, you're nev - er a - lone, you know. ____ Just think of your

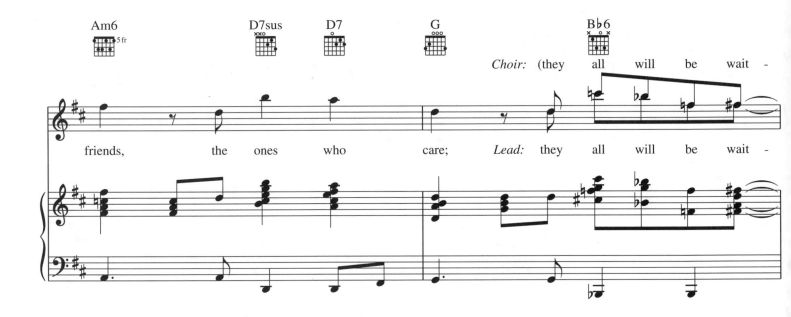

friends, the ones who care; *Lead:* they all will be wait -

Choir: (they all will be wait -

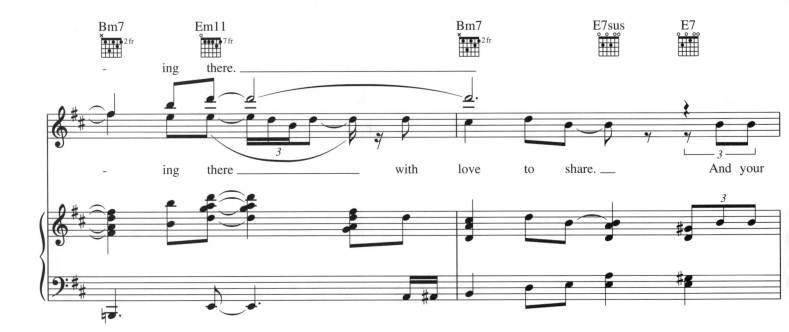

- ing there ____ with love to share. ____ And your

- ing there. ____

MOULIN ROUGE

Original Music: Craig Armstrong, David Bowie,
   Marius De Vries, Steve Hitchcock, Elton John,
   Kimberly "Lil Kim" Jones; with songs by
   various others
Screenplay: Baz Luhrmann and Craig Pearce
Produced by: Fred Andrews, Martin Brown, Baz
   Luhrman for Bazmark Films
Directed by: Baz Luhrmann
Cinematography: Donald McAlpine (DeLuxe)
Cast: Nicole Kidman, Ewan McGregor, Jim
   Broadbent, John Leguizamo, Richard Roxburgh
Songs: "Lady Marmalade"; "Because We Can";
   "Sparkling Diamonds"; "Timbaland"; "Children of
   the Revolution"; "Nature Boy"; "Le Tango de Roxanne";
   "One Day I'll Fly Away"; "Rhythm of the Night"; "Hindi
   Sad Diamonds"; "Your Song"; "Elephant Love";
   "Come What May"; "Compliante de la Butte"
Released: May 2001; 127 minutes

Nicole Kidman and Ewan McGregor.

Blurring the lines between the Hollywood musical and MTV, *Moulin Rouge* is a tragic love story told before a dizzying background of song and dance. Set in the cultural revolution on the eve of the twentieth century, the story finds a young English writer named Christian (Ewan McGregor) defying his parents and moving to Paris. He immediately connects with a Toulouse-Lautrec (John Leguizamo) and a band of bohemians devoted to "truth, beauty, freedom—and above all—love," and sets out to write a show for the Moulin Rouge. He tries to pitch the show to the Moulin Rouge's most famous performer/courtesan, Satine (Nicole Kidman), who mistakes him for a Duke she is to seduce in hopes of winning his investment in a new show. Christian and Satine fall in love, just as the Duke agrees to invest if Satine becomes his alone. In the end all lose as the Duke is rejected and Satine dies of consumption on opening night of the new show – in the arms of Christian. But the film is less about the love story than is an excuse for whirling, frenetic song-and-dance sequences constructed of an anachronistic mix of period trappings and a seemingly endless stream of late twentieth-century pop/rock tunes.

Bazmark Films 20th Century Fox

Come What May
FROM MOULIN ROUGE

Words and Music by
DAVID BAERWALD

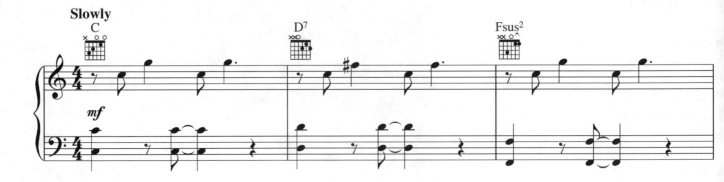

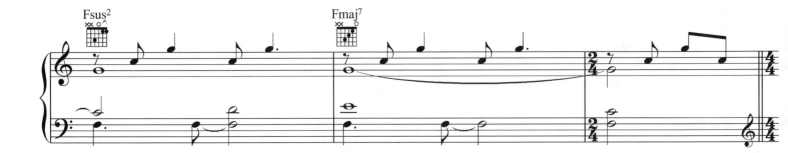

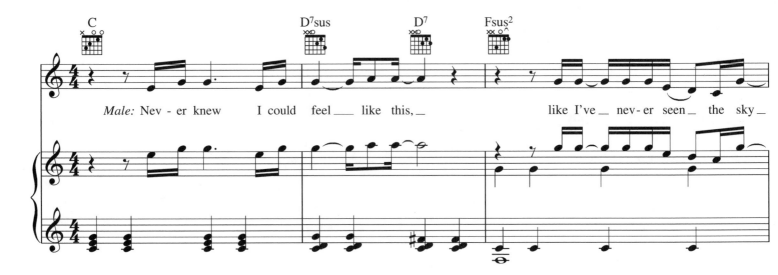

Male: Nev-er knew I could feel __ like this, __ like I've nev-er seen __ the sky __

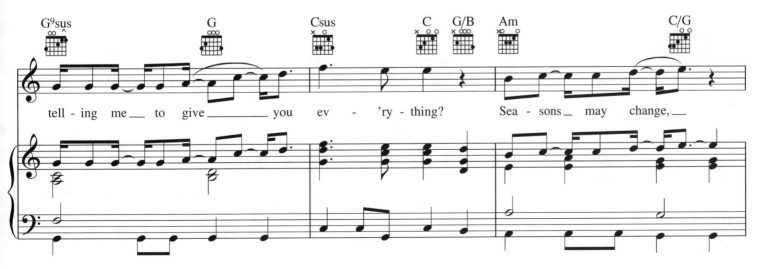

win - ter to spring, but I love you un - til the

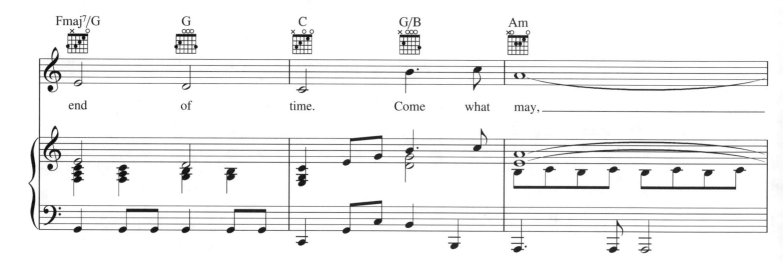

end of time. Come what may, _____

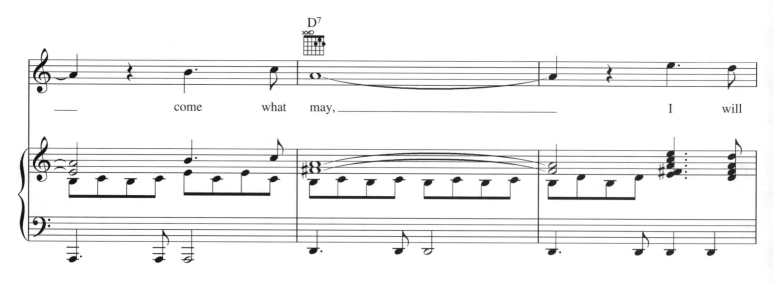

_____ come what may, _____ I will

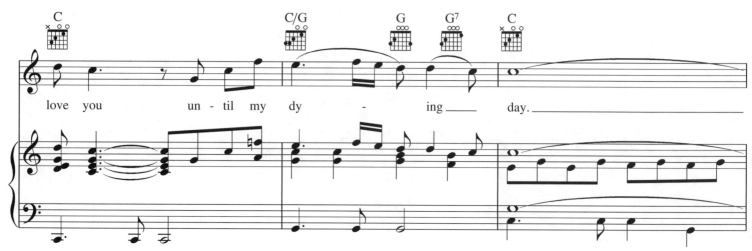

love you un - til my dy - ing _____ day.

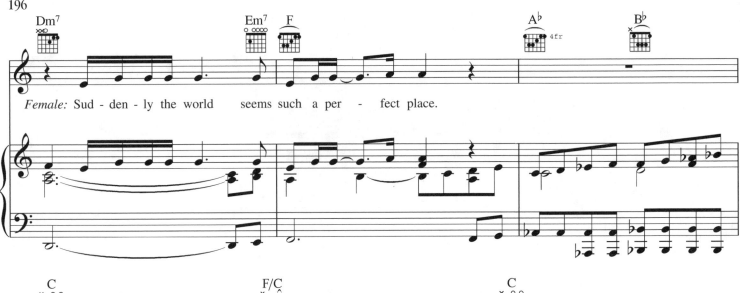

Female: Sud - den - ly the world seems such a per - fect place.

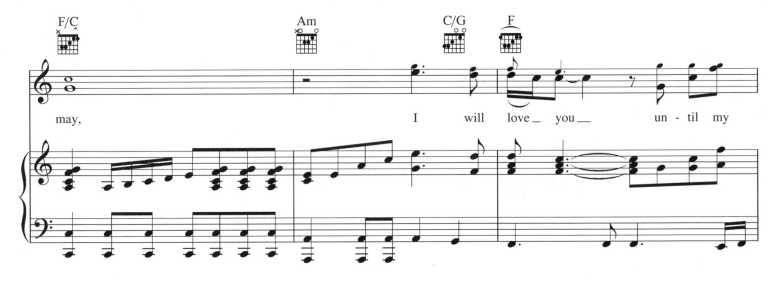

Both: Come what may, come what

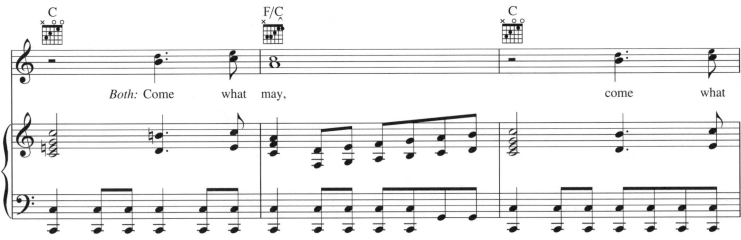

may, I will love_ you_ un - til my

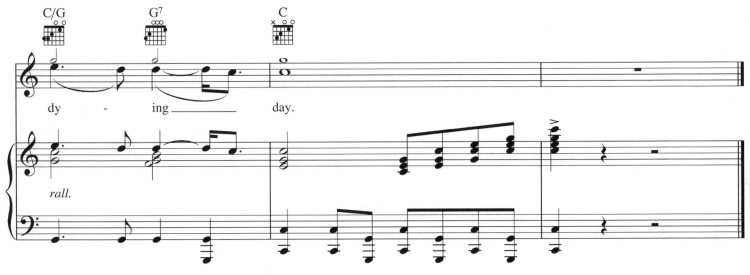

dy - ing_____ day.

rall.

One Day I'll Fly Away

FROM MOULIN ROUGE

Words and Music by WILL JENNINGS
and JOE SAMPLE

What more could your love do for me? When will love be through with me?

Why live life from dream to dream, and _ dread the day when _

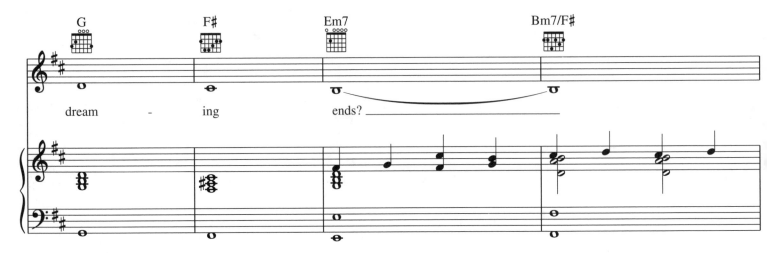

dream - ing ends? _____

With growing intensity

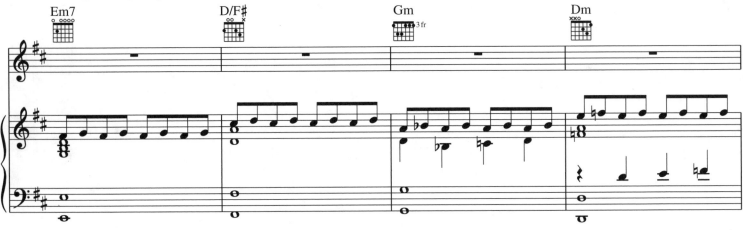